Fog City Review

Winter 2008

Special Dedication To:

John Fichera (1934-2007)
Edward Simpson (1936-2007)

Fog City Review
A Literary Review

<u>Editors</u>

Editor in Chief

Steven Fichera

Advisory Editors

Michael Borbone   Katie Ramos
Hamilton Burrows   Adam Slote
Jieyi Cui   Julie Wood

Fog City Review is published biannually. All correspondence should be directed to Fog City Writers, 350 Bay Street, Suite 100-348, San Francisco, CA 94133-1966. Visit our website at: www.fogcitywriters.com. Submissions must be emailed to submissions@fogcitywriters.com.   We no longer accept submissions via U.S. Mail. We cannot assume responsibility for any works that fail to reach our inbox. We do not print footnotes.

2161_4

ISBN 978-1-58909-433-8

Printed in the United States of America

Cover Designed by: Jieyi Cui

Contents

Volume One * Number One
Winter 2008

~

Short Fiction

Angela Kriger Blackwood
Working Title
3

Dawsen Wright Albertsen
The Sheets Hang Limp
9

Jackie Shannon-Hollis
The Words That Would Fix This Thing
17

Lynn Veach Sadler
Six Degrees of Juicy
27

Donna Trump
Wolf
41

Ruth Lilian
The First Wife
53

Beverly Akerman
Sea of Tranquility
65

Gilda Haber
Tea with the Editor
75

Sharon E. Mortz
M&Ms
89

Michael John Paul Pope
Blink
97

Randy Susan Meyers
Mixed Prayers
111

Poetry

Ysabel de la Rosa
Art
126

J. D. Blair
One More Day
127

Ginna Wilkerson
Ginna in the Silence
128

La Specola
Stephanie A. Amsel
129

Piero Scaruffi
Elegy of the Witness – The Same River Twice
130

J. George Hume
Let Your Soul Rise
132

Floyd E. Batchelder
Maudie and Claude
134

Valerie Stokes
Three Poems
136

Anthony Russell White
February Morning, Vashon Island
143

About the Authors
145

Short Fiction

WORKING TITLE

~

Angela Kriger Blackwood

I fling the crumpled ball of paper against the wall in anger and frustration and wait for the satisfying smack as it hits the hard surface. But I hear nothing but the unending silence. The absolute silence. My arm drops to my side as I stare into the emptiness—an expanse of emptiness deeper than nothingness. The wall that stood before me only moments ago has vanished and I glance down to see the paper fading quickly as well. The void is closing in again.

No... no, you don't..." I focus my thoughts on the paper, willing it back into existence and watch, satisfied, as it begins to take shape again almost instantly. I raise my head, empowered by my small success, and start visualizing the wall again, my eyes screwed tightly shut to keep the oppressive emptiness at bay.

"Still at it, are you?" a hollow voice speaks from behind me. My concentration is broken, and I struggle to contain my anger and frustration at the interruption.

"Go away, I'm working. I can do this. I just need time—time to figure things out." I turn to the intruder. "There was a time you believed in me, Randall," I remark with a hint of reproach.

"Why don't you take a break now? You've been away from the rest of us for ages," he hesitates and looks away, "And I've told you before not to call me Randall—I don't like it. I shouldn't have a name, it's wrong. It's unnatural."

"It's unnatural for us to *not* have names," I counter defiantly. "Anyway, I like the name Randall. Randall was my best friend. Before..."

I turn my attention back to the paper that had been only moments from becoming a reality, but I see that it has vanished entirely. My attention has wavered for too long. With a sigh I stand and watch as my chair fades into the void and I feel the self-identity I had dedicated myself to creating once again evaporate into a cold, misty shadow of nothingness.

Randall and I leave what was once the compartment I had struggled for so long to create, and enter what is now just another part of the noisy common area where everyone else exists, awaiting their selection. While I crave independence and solitude, these others fear seclusion and shrink from individuality. It is far easier to congregate and wallow in a mass of sameness until their time comes to leave. I am nothing like these shadows.

"Look at them," I sneer, "so dependent on others for life, adventure, form. They're nothing but blank sheets just waiting to become what others define them as. They disgust me."

Randall glances at me, almost, but not quite sorrowfully. "You have to accept that you're one of us. You're nothing but a character without a story; you can't continue this pretense of being someone. You can't make yourself into something you've never been," he states without emotion, our figures melting into the spiritless mass of the others around us.

I remain silent, recognizing the pointlessness of argument. It isn't Randall's fault that I am different. He isn't capable of understanding why I feel such a need for individuality, why I want so badly to create a life for myself—to salvage the promise of the vibrant and meaningful life that I'd been tempted with so long ago.

I am a cast-off character. I've been relegated to this purgatory of nonexistence, where even time cannot be measured, with very little hope of ever being fully developed or seeing my story completed.

There was a time when I was a main character—a protagonist nonetheless. I was destined for excitement, failure, the hero's quest, heartache, love, and ultimately, greatness. Millions should have loved me—should have been inspired by me. People should have named their children after me. I should have been the subject of decades of research papers, scholars dissecting my every utterance, my every move. But my story became tangled and confused and it has languished for years, unfinished, frozen in my author's memory, and filed away, deep in the recesses of his mind.

Over time, each of the other characters from my story found new lives in re-imagined plots and situations as my author continued to hone his craft, but I remained in the original manuscript, too powerful and exceptional to be wasted in just any plot. I deserved better and so I was set aside, intended for something great—I was meant for a masterpiece. However, time has a way of passing by relentlessly, and the motivation necessary to create my tour de force has yet to arrive.

Though I was never completely forgotten, I have been stored away for so long that I have lost hope that my author will ever complete me. In time, I was forced to return here, to this dreary holding cell, semi-developed with my own will and disposition far beyond the others that wait here with me. Though I was given my own idiosyncrasies and ambitions, outside of a story they serve no purpose. I am expected to remain here in this nowhere, waiting passively until someday an author thinks of me and sees my potential and at last my destiny will be fulfilled, and I will be rescued from this eternal waiting. The cruelty of being created with the promise of such literary and cultural significance and then expected to waste away in this place is beyond my comprehension. I have tried to take control of my own destiny and at times I seem so close to being able to create my own reality. But each taste of victory is followed by a crushing failure and the void always surges back.

I am lost in my thoughts, when Randall speaks again, interrupting my reverie. "Did you hear? A character was chosen yesterday. The odd one—he was always lurking in corners and creeping in the shadows. He's gone to a horror novel. There's gossip that he was a stock character—just dropped him right into the plot, easy as pie! We should all be so lucky... It's perfect for him, though, don't you think? Not likely that he'll end up back here!" Randall laughs.

I glare at him, knowing he means well, but I've grown so tired of the repetitive jokes about how I arrived here, well developed but abandoned, and no longer generic enough to be chosen for just any new story.

Randall attempts to keep me occupied, but his dialog is stilted and lifeless and I am quickly bored with his meaningless, run on sentences. "I'm going back now," I finally interject. For the briefest of moments he looks hurt by my abruptness, but being incapable of any lasting emotion he turns away and melts into the crowd.

I push through the mass of grey shapes, a frisson of revulsion overtaking me, as it often does, knowing that I am more like these non-beings than I care to admit. It is demoralizing to confront the sure knowledge that I have very little chance of ever leaving this place. I can appreciate the fact that an author wants a character that he or she can create, cultivate, and mold to fit a story, not a character that has already been semi-constructed and has his own well-formed agendas and traits.

Eventually I find myself in a quiet area with nothing else to do but try once more to expand my own existence. I focus on recreating my chair and desk and then the paper and pencil I'd been using before Randall's interruption. It seems I have spent an eternity in these attempts to establish my identity through my own writing, but I can never produce anything permanent. I always return to this shadowy form, a nearly lifeless character attempting to give myself the gift of life the only way I've ever known. I put my pencil to the paper and begin again, just as I have done countless other times.

Pace scratches away at the blank page, finding an escape in his writing—a relief from the monotony to which he's been condemned.

I pause for a moment to read what I have just written. I realize that these scribblings will never inspire rave reviews or invitations to speak at book clubs, but for now I only want a life, a reality.

His pencil trembles as he continues his work, the lines on the page blurring as his focus wavers.

I let out a sigh of annoyance. This is what always happens, I can only write about what I *am* doing never what I *want* to do or think. I close my eyes, reaching within myself to find the will to continue with this seemingly futile experiment. I open my eyes again and re-read the lines, surprised to see more on the page than what I have just written.

He wants so much to be away from this place, to be back in a story, his story. To someday have a life—a reality. But it he is now accepting that it will never happen. He has often thought about finding an alternate end, a more permanent end, but he has never attempted it. Now, the idea is entering his mind again and is finding a much more welcome reception than it ever has before. He feels the long forgotten sensations of decision and resolve that he has not experienced since he came into existence long, long ago

I think about what I have just read, and realize with a disturbing combination of fear and relief that it is true. I have often contemplated taking the route that is currently playing out in my mind, but how? I watch the page, waiting for more, but nothing appears. I take up my pencil again, more thoughtfully this time, and write.

The death of a character is a curious thing. When there is a death in fiction, it isn't truly a death as long as the character remains in the memories of those who have read its story. Pace considers these things carefully as he searches for answers. In his case, he is the only one who can remember who he is... or was. But what if he can convince himself that he never existed? What if he can forget that he was ever written? It has become apparent to him over time that he is incapable of giving himself a reality, but could he be capable of taking reality away?

I glance at my pencil and see that it is fading ever so slowly. Instead of refocusing to bring it back, I quickly return to my writing, before it is gone.

He watches as the things around him—the things he has worked so hard to create—begin to vanish. He is aware that this time feels different; it isn't the void closing in to erase his limited reality. Now his entire world is darkening, curling, and disappearing into a vapor and he finally understands that there is no effort he can make to restore his reality. As substance and memories diminish he begins to feel lighter, different. He had never realized how tired he was; how much his half-life had strained him. The sentences he has written barely show as he stares in puzzlement at the paper lying before him. The pencil is gone now…

***

The old man sits in the wheelchair that has been his prison for the last few years of his life. The passage of time has eroded his body and now it has begun to affect his mind. But the one memory of his great novel that never materialized and its main character still haunts him. He had always assumed that there would be more time and that someday inspiration would strike, but now he knows that time has run out. His memories have begun to fade more rapidly and he has come to terms with the certainty that his masterpiece will never be written. Still, the character haunts his thoughts, even from the depths of the cabinet that hasn't been touched in years.

He directs the girl to the dusty grey filing cabinet, hidden out of sight in the shadows of his office. She attempts to open the drawer that he indicated, but struggles with the rusted tracks, and wonders how long it has been since her grandfather had closed it last. Inside the drawer, she sees only a small pile of old yellowing pages. The handwritten, once black ink has faded to a mottled brown over the years, as the pages lay untouched in the drawer.

The man smiles sadly as she carefully lifts the papers and walks back to him, holding before him the last of his life's dreams. He looks at his old work for a moment, but cannot bring himself to take it from her. He thinks fondly of the characters he had created so many years ago, particularly of the one that has remained with him for so long, a character so full of life, a character far too great for any other work he'd ever written. Unable to do his character justice he had locked him away, always waiting for the perfect story. Now he is dying, and the hope for the great story will die with him.

He nods weakly and closes his eyes, unable to watch the final chapter unfolding before him. The girl bites her lip, momentarily resisting the request her grandfather has made of her. She knows that it is something he must do, and something that he can only accomplish with her help, but as she turns away from her grandfather, memories of the enchanting stories he told her throughout her childhood are flooding back. Even now, witnessing him in his most fragile state, she marvels at the gift he has always had to bring his characters to life. She knows that this stack of papers was meant to be his most extraordinary story and as she carries the brittle bundle to the fire, burning brightly in the small fireplace, she feels a deep pang of regret that she will never know what lives are buried its pages.

She looks back at her grandfather, needing his assurance once more that this is what he truly wants. She sees that his eyes are tightly shut, a small tear just in the corner of one eye, so, resigned to her promise, she turns back to the fireplace to carry out his request. She watches as the flames devour the papers, feeling her grandfather's palpable grief as the dry pages flare up instantly and the words turn to smoke. Blind to the scene playing out in his presence, the old man listens to the crackling of the flames, relinquishing the life that he had given his characters so many years ago, allowing them to at last slip into the void that he felt finally tugging at his own frail existence.

The Sheets Hang Limp

~

Dawsen Wright Albertsen

The sheets hang limp. They billow from the wind. They are limp again. Sarah could sit watching them until they dried. She enjoys them nearly still and almost motionless but prefers they move and shake. They should flap as flags and as pennants. They should roll as hills and bluffs along rivers and streams. And they should sound with cracks and claps and snaps and if lucky soft light thunders. They were already white. The sheets were a sick yellow a few minutes ago. "What time is it?" she thinks. Sarah lifts her cell phone from the windowsill. The screen lights. "It can't be two," she thinks, "of course the sheets are white." Sarah has sat watching them for over an hour. "Damn it, Michael," she says.

A family across the yards also hangs their sheets today. Those sheets are still smoky yellow. "Bad teeth," Sarah thinks. "I'll have those teeth," she says. She flicks her right canine. Sarah tongues the face of her upper teeth. "If I continue using Michael's shitty toothpaste," she thinks.

Half Wednesday elapses. She watched and she watches and she will watch the sheets. The sheets hang. The sheets flap. The sheets roll from the clothesline. "I hate that smell though," Sarah says. "Mildewy, fabric softener, mildewy, not mildewy, what is that smell," Sarah thinks. "Ew, God," she says. She wonders how she agreed with Michael to hang the laundry.

A small woman wearing faded powder blue track pants and a white t-shirt climbs half-out a window. The woman draws in one of her sheets. "They're still wet, dumb- dumb," Sarah says. The woman returns the sheets to hang.

Sarah knew not this petulance. They are not her sheets. The sheets belong to track pants woman. Sarah does not know the track pants woman. She does not want to know her. But she wonders why she is bothered. He isn't here. He did nothing. He had done nothing. He hadn't done anything. "Exactly," she says. She sucks air like dragging a cigarette. She exhales no smoke. "Not a thing. He and his wind-dried sheets. They kind of hang and billow like a dress," she thinks, "maybe an apron. Big lady. Fat man. Michael needs to exercise."

"Fuck," she says, "Bobo." Over her left shoulder she sees Bobo. He lies on his flannel bed. The chocolate Lab sprawls his one-hundred fifty pounds across the bed as he sleeps. His belly rises and falls like a bubble that never bursts. "Walk him later," she says. Sarah pictures walking Bobo around the block. He will stop to piss on the sewer grate. He won't lift his leg. He will piss on his front paws. He may shit between the tree and the hydrant. Then he will hurry home, to sleep. "God he's fat," she thinks. The sheets curl and roll. Bobo sneezes. "Bless you," she says. A sheet cracks in the wind.

"Maybe her sheets are yellow," she thinks. Sarah imagines the faded blue track pants becoming wet as the woman lightly scrubs dishes, splattering water about her front, the counter and the floor; falling cherries burning small black holes in the track pants as the woman smokes and pushes a vacuum cleaner while soap operas blare; the track pants scrunch as she bunches the sheets into a bucket of cold water and soap where they are left to sit until she remembers to hang them to dry. "Bad housekeeping," she thinks, "I don't know."

If there were wind it avoids her sheets and the yellow sheets. Nothing is animated. "This is boring," she says. She stands and walks to Bobo. Bobo lightly snores and drools heavily on his bed. "Bobo," she startles him. He looks at Sarah with mouth agape and drool sagging to the bed. She pets his back, his side, his belly. She tickles him. He stares at her with dopey tired eyes. "Yes, now," she says. Bobo rolls onto his back leaving his paws in the air. She yanks the leash and collar from the coat rack hook. Bobo stands, stretches and shakes. "So, you want to go," she says. Bobo sits. He wags his tail. The wind blows. The sheets dance. She thinks, "we'll go later." She tells Bobo, "we'll go later." She hangs the leash and collar on the hook. She returns and sits in the chair in front the window. Bobo lies on the bed. She watches the sheets.

"I really can't tell," she thinks, "maybe they are turning white. Michael would know." She imagines Michael speaking with an English accent dandily affected with spats, quirt and fob, "they remind one of a smoked albatross egg that happened to roll through pancake batter to sit and dry on a white sand beach early one Sunday morning as the sun blanches it, one early April Sunday morning, that is." Sarah smirks at her exaggeration of Michael. The not yet white and the not yellow sheets snap from the wind. "Know-it-all," she says. She shakes her head and thinks, "smash those eggs in his face." She laughs while picturing the rotten eggs. Sulfuric fumes choke Michael as rotten yolks and putrid whites drip down his face. "Oh," she says, "that's just mad."

Bobo's wet nose touches her elbow. He licks her once and sits. "It's okay, Bobo," she says. Bobo rests his head on her side. "Maybe they're sunburned," she thinks, "like the windowsill or an old newspaper." A thousand off-whites pass her mind. She pets Bobo but watches the sheets, the sheets and the yards.

Two cats, one black and one grey, cross the tarpapered garage's roof. "Bobo, you were that small," she says, "once." The cats vanish with the breeze that tussles her sheets. Then she notices Bobo's size. "You were so small. You were… one-fifteenth? one-twentieth your size?" she thinks. Bobo licks the side of her jeans. "Oh my," she says, "my God. Eight fucking years." She realizes it was nine years ago that she met Michael. Eight and one half years ago they moved to Brooklyn. Seven years ago they moved again. They moved into this railroad apartment. The apartment has one decent view. The view is hanging, drying and billowing clothes, towels and sheets. The kitchen offers that view. "What have we done?" she says. A strange, an unknown sadness flushes her. The apple red cheeks pale. The paleness is lighter than her sheets, lighter than the whiteness she wants her teeth to shine. She, they, she and Michael had done nothing criminal, nothing morally repugnant; nothing considered a social faux pas. She is embarrassed. She knows not why. But again, she misspoke. An error she commonly performs. 'Where has the time gone' she articulated as 'what have we done'. "We've done nothing," she says. She affirms herself correct and shakes her head. Sarah picks up the phone. She rolls it in her right hand. The face lights. She wants to call. But there is no one to call. There is not someone. There is no one with whom to talk. There is nothing to say to that someone, to that no one. What would she say? She says, "no, nothing, nothing wrong." She lay the phone on the windowsill. A light breeze shimmies her sheets as the neighbor's sheets hang limp. "An asshole could say that's a crime, but that were another time, before our time," she thinks. "Now," she thinks, 'as Michael would say,' "now, now doing the least damage is doing the greatest good." She assures herself of this, of their good. Sarah and Michael did less by hanging their sheets. They do more. "We do good," she says.

"Are you my child?" she asks Bobo. Her tone resonates through the fat Lab. His tail wags as if to break from his body. "Of course you are," she says. They kiss. Sarah puckers and Bobo licks her face. "But it's nine years," she thinks. The sheets hang limp. There is no wind. But Sarah thinks that there is a wind, a wind that evades every sheet.

"They are yellow," she thinks. She compares her sheets to their sheets: white – off-white, white – yellow, not-white white – not-yellow yellow, not-white – not-yellow, wet – wet. "Don't you want kids to play with?" she asks Bobo. Gust and gusts of wind blow the sheets to billow, to undulate, to lie atop imaginary beds, parallel the ground. One, two, three, four, five, six, six beds float. "I could watch this all day," she says. Bobo lies at her side. The dog sighs. Sarah laughs. The sheet nearest the window crackles. The wind snaps the sheet up and outward from the line. Sarah startles.

The woman in the blue track pants climbs half-out her window. She draws in the sheet. She draws the sheet out again. "Of course they're wet," Sarah says, "it's been five minutes." Sarah sighs. "God, you're like Michael, now, now, now," Sarah thinks, "well, kind of, sort of, sort of not at all." Sarah crosses her legs, she crosses them again, and again and again. She uncrosses her legs and leans back in the chair. "Five-year engagement," she says, "oh that's pretty." The sheets billow a wave, both marine and sporting. "Has it been three years?" she thinks. "No… we went. We were at Shea… one, two, Jesus it was three. Oh my. It has." She reaches toward Bobo; she wants to pet him, to touch him. He is not there. He lies on his bed with his paws in the air.

"They seem to dance," she thinks. The track pants lady is at her window. She stretches, then lights a cigarette and smokes. "Come on, dumb-dumb," Sarah says, "they'll smell like smoke." Sarah focuses on the woman: cheeks narrow, then smoke erupts from her mouth until it dissipates. "It's been almost four years," she thinks, "that's pretty good. Now and then one wouldn't be bad. Not with kids, no, never with kids." Sarah considers running to the corner store. "One pack," she thinks, "Michael would probably have some."

Sarah thinks about college. She remembers her early twenties with nights spent at shows, bars, parties, clubs, openings, with random girls and guys. Names of artists, writers, actors, philosophers, critics, musicians, and common celebrities flood her mind. Those she adored and idolized. Those who inspired and whom she aspired to become. She thinks about thinking, creating, doing, and simply wanting to do more. "I used to think," she says, "I did." She watches the sheets dance like marionettes.

"Am I going to sit here all day?" she thinks, "I'll take Bobo at four. Bobo. Why did I agree to that? Jesus, Michael. Bobo. The shit I've done. Whatever. It's a name. It is only a name. Bobo the big fat clown." Bobo looks at Sarah. She winks at him. "Aren't you, Bobo?

Yes you are," she says. She walks to his bed. She crouches and pets Bobo's back and side. Bobo lies still. Sarah returns to the window.

"We need more color," she says, "someone should hang some pinks and blues, some greens and reds, some yellows... there are yellows." She giggles. Sarah stares at the neighbor's sheets. She does not blink. Light spiders, as Sarah calls them, dance about her eyes. They dart over the sheets and buildings. She blinks. She feels Bobo lick her elbow. The light spiders are gone. "No. Some pastels would be nice. I like this," she says, "I do. I don't know why, but some colors would be nice." Sarah tugs on Bobo's ear. She folds it and pinches it. She musses his crown. "Should we wash some colorful sheets, Bobo?" she says. "Not until these dry," Sarah thinks.

Sarah looks at the rooftops. For years she has wanted a rooftop deck. She imagines sitting atop the building drinking beer and reading, drinking lemonade and reading, drinking tea, wine, scotch, margaritas. "When does he come home, Bobo?" she asks, "all these new jobs. That's why, Bobo." A shadow has crept across the neighbor's sheet closest to the building. Bobo returns to his bed. "I don't want to," she thinks, "pull these in, fold them up, put them away and make the bed."

A grey haired woman in a pea green housedress climbs onto a fire escape. The woman clips brightly colored toddlers' shirts and pants to the line until a series of miniature tops and bottoms hang across the yard. "It's too late, lady," Sarah says, "they'll never dry by night." But the red shirt, blue pants, green shirt, brown pants, red and white barred shirt, tiny brown corduroys, and blue oxford make Sarah smile.

"Martha," screams an old woman. Sarah searches for the voice's body. The woman on the fire escape yells, "hi, Mary." Then Sarah sees a tiny hunched brown floral dressed woman in the yard next to the building where 'Martha' hovers. Mary waves then yells, "what are you doing?" Mary shades her eyes with her left hand. Her right hand flings into the air, hanging, and waiting. She draws in that hand to create a larger visor as she stares at Martha. "I'm doing laundry, Mary. What does it look like I'm doing?" Martha says. Mary throws out her hands. Martha throws up her hands. "What are you doing?" asks Martha. "Sheets," replies Mary. But Mary doesn't hang any sheets. Mary returns inside the building. Martha vanishes into the window. Sarah waits. She waits for Mary to return. She hopes Mary will bring some color to the view. She hopes Mary will hang pastels. Mary may hang gigantic brightly colored sheets. Sarah concentrates on her grandmother's house. "What did gamma use?" she asks. Bobo's ears perk and he rises. "White," she says, "plain old white." Bobo lies to sleep. She muses and wonders what colors Mary uses for bedding.

Then Sarah notices there are not clotheslines over Mary's yard. Not one line runs from the first, second, third, or fourth floor to the post. "She's nuts," she says, "Mary's flipped, Bobo, she's flipped." Sarah giggles. She shakes her head. Her face reddens with embarrassment. Sarah shoots a finger pistol in the air. "Washer-dryer," she says.

Wind rips through the yards. Sheets soar like magic carpets without riders. The miniature tops and bottoms dance, bounce and fly. Sarah's three sheets crack and furl, snap and rise, lower and boom. It calms. All fall, hang and silence. The sheets are limp and lifeless.

Bobo snores. He seems to gurgle every breath. "Maybe he'll dream," Sarah thinks, wanting to watch him wriggle and muffle-bark. "That's stupid," she says, "he's probably dreaming now." Sarah fumes, she curses herself, she thinks about sleeping and dreaming, "do I quiver and mumble?" she wonders. Bobo snores, he does not bark in his sleep, his paws are not wriggling, his muzzle does not puff, swell and deflate. He snores. He is not chasing his dreams, dreaming squirrels.

Sarah has never witnessed a tornado or a hurricane. She imagines the sheets behaving in each storm. How would they dance? "A schottische," she says. She snorts a laugh imagining the sheets, Michael, track pants lady, herself, Mary, and Martha dancing about the yards. Hundreds of clogged quartets bouncing and caroming from building to building, from sheet to sheet, rooftop to cloud. There are no clouds. "They all fall down," she says. The wind does blow. And the sheets furl and curl and roll and cower and slap and fuss. "But no, they dance," she thinks, watching the sheets float. She imagines the fat apron man and large dress woman happily kicking their hems into the air. The children fly in halves. A few swim backstroke in the air. Others glide and soar like superman. They dangle. They slacken. They hang. "Oh that's awful," says Sarah. The neighbor's sheets wink. She winces at their behavior. "Brusque," she thinks, "burlesque. Burlesque dancers. What a mistake." She kicks the wall beneath the windowsill, she asks, "why did I go?"

"Stop it," she yells. Bobo quits digging and scratching his bed. "When did you wake up?" she asks. Bobo lumbers toward her dragging his nose along the floor. He licks her elbow. She pats his crown. His tail wags excitedly. She cups his head with her hands. Sarah puckers and Bobo licks her lips and nose. Bobo lies at her feet. He sighs. "Soon Bobo," she says, "we'll go out soon."

"Maybe they are white," she thinks. The neighbor's sheets seem to whiten. Each sheet seems lighter in the creeping shadow.

Sarah likes living on the short side of the block. She sees more. More buildings, more windows, more fire escapes, and more clotheslines are available to view. There are more sheets to watch, more sheets to hang and toss about the air. If she lived on the long side she couldn't see as much. Twelve buildings line the west, nine line the east, three line the south, and four line the north on the corner of which dwell Sarah and Michael among seven other apartments. Sarah wonders if anyone watches her sheets, as she watches the neighbor's sheets. Sarah looks to her left. She scans every window of every building. Near the Southeast corner she cannot see windows. She thinks about binoculars. The southern buildings are too far. Five buildings north of the south she can see again. She scans every window. She sees no one. "Oh no, Bobo," says Sarah, "I'm a peeper." Bobo sits upright and looks at Sarah. "Oh well," she thinks, "no one watches but me." He lies, resting his head on his forepaws.

Sarah's sheets whip, thunder and clap. They startle her and Bobo. The neighbor's sheets try flying from their clothesline. Sarah hopes one will escape.

"Blizzard," Sarah exclaims. A hazy frost covers the yards, she imagines, a light snow and low temperatures freezing the sheets. Then wind cracking the sheets as ice and drift explode from each sheet. She smiles at this imaginary howling wind that freezes one sheet and tears it in two. The pinned half is pelted by the wind as the other half flies like a kite into the sky, leaving the yards. Bobo prances to the door. He sniffs under the door. He stands and paws the knob.

Michael enters the apartment. He closes the door with his shoulder. The humidity engorges the door and jamb. Michael throws his body into the door again. The door clicks. Sarah stares at the sheets.

"Hey," he says. Bobo stands and licks Michael's chin. Michael holds Bobo's forepaws and lowers him to the ground.

"Hi," she says.

"What's going on?" he asks. Bobo walks in circles, rubbing Michael's legs. Michael steps left of Bobo.

"You know," she says, "laundry." The sheets hang limp. No breeze stirs a sheet, a shirt, a pant leg, a wire, a twig, a leaf. But she watches the stillness. Bobo walks between Michael's legs.

"They look dry," he says. Michael steps over and right of Bobo.

"I haven't fucking had time," she yells.

"I didn't…" he begins. Bobo walks behind Michael while his wagging tail brushes Michael's legs.

"I've been busy," she says, "okay?" Bobo sits. He looks at Sarah, and then stares at Michael.

Michael stares at her, her hair's part, and then follows the brown curls to their end hanging beneath the chairs back. She sits motionless. She does not turn. She does not face him. He spies the apartment. He looks for change, for new, for signs of a cleaning rampage. Sarah always leaves signs, little tells detailing her chore. A wet mop stands in the corner. A paintbrush drips colored water onto newspaper as it rests on a paint can under the sink. A wet towel lay beside Bobo's bed. A feast adorns the table. Sandpaper, lacquer, brushes sit beside a dark and sticky chair. An entire room is rearranged except one piece not yet placed. Today, there is no sign. The apartment is the same as the morning. There is no telling detail.

"What did you do?" he asks. Bobo walks once around Michael without touching him. He sits and wags his tail.

"Stop it," she says, "it's been a long day."

Michael waits. All is quiet. This pause is longer than the day he just worked. "What," he thinks, "how." Bobo whimpers.

"We should bring them in soon," he says.

"Okay," she says.

"I'll do it. I'll bring them in," he says, "think about what you want to eat."

"No," she says, "not yet."

Bobo returns to his bed. He sighs. He lies and stares at Michael's shoes.

"Not yet what?" he asks.

"The sheets," she says.

"Well, tell me when," he says.

"No," she says, "I will bring them in, I will fold them, I will make the bed."

Bobo yawns loudly. He stands, twice circles clockwise then lies.

"Seriously Sarah," Michael says, "I'll do it."

"No, no. I'll do it," she says. All the sheets roll and whip and wave their tails. Sarah giggles. "They're not done yet," she says.

The Words That Would Fix This Thing

~

Jackie Shannon-Hollis

On the Sunday that Paul and Dee went through the things of their marriage, to decide who got what, Carl and I took their son on a hike up the gorge. Paul and Dee meant to have any of the bickering that came of the divvying all decided by the time we got back with Nick. When we left them on their porch in the city, Paul was rubbing his face with both hands and Dee had her jaw set like it was fixed in cement. My husband Carl was driving. He turned the corner and we couldn't see Paul and Dee any more. Carl said "Oh, God," so quiet I wasn't sure I heard it, or whether he even knew he'd said it.

Nick was in the back seat, his legs stretched out clear to the opposite door. That's how big he'd gotten. He was sixteen and the little boy of him was almost completely gone. He listened to music on his iPod and looked mostly at the tiny screen there, hardly ever looking at the road ahead, or at the Columbia, the river that ran next to the freeway. The white cords from the ear buds trailed down the front of his blue t-shirt, which was soft and faded and had frays at the neck. Nick had always been a boy who got attached to a piece of clothing and Dee would have to talk him into taking the thing off for a cleaning (the pajama bottoms with a sail boat print, the New York Yankee's baseball cap he got from a trip with his dad, a braided wrist band we'd brought him from Mexico). This blue shirt had the look of that, of something favorite, but we didn't see Nick as often these days, so it was hard to know.

For the forty-five minutes up the Columbia Gorge, Nick didn't say a word. He thumbed through the music on his iPod and either ignored or didn't hear Carl and I making talk we hoped would pull him in. It was the middle of October. It had rained the day before, but on that Sunday the sky was the crisp clear that Oregon gives as a gift only in the fall. Nick wasn't appreciating that.

Partway there, I reached to put a Kleenex in the trash bag that hung on the back of the seat. My arm brushed against Nick's knee, the coarse hair there. I pulled my hand back quick, but not before Nick's head snapped up and he moved his leg in a fast way, like he was taking something back.

Earlier in the summer we'd helped Paul and Dee put a new lawn in their yard. It had been a while since we'd seen Paul and Dee, and longer since we'd seen Nick because, over the last few years, his friends had taken a bigger place in his life. That day, putting the sod in, was before Paul and Dee's divorce was anything we even knew could be a possibility.

It got warm and we were all running sweat. Nick pulled off his t-shirt and my eyes kept coming back to him. The way his chest had filled out. To the flat of his stomach. The small trail of hair that started below his naval and disappeared under the band of his shorts. It had all happened so fast and it made me shy, not sure of myself with him. Over the last few years, I'd already lost the easy way I had with Nick, how I used to tickle him or pull him onto my lap. But now it was this, something more to get used to, the way his voice had deepened and his body had gone from boy thin to something else, something more like a man. I had to make myself look away and it wasn't the sun that brought out the redness in my face.

But then in the heat of that early summer day, when we took a break for lunch, Carl did the same dumb joke he always did with Nick: stuck something, this time it was two grapes but it could have been anything (a French fry, a pickle) up his nose and turned to Nick. Carl kept on with the most serious conversation he could muster. It was in that moment I saw Nick's old grin, the wide one that made two little creases on each side of his mouth and opened up to a chuckle. Nick's chuckle, like two small hoots of an owl, was followed by the bigger laugh, big strong hoots, that had kept Carl going all these years, doing those silly things. It was the laugh I'd first heard from Nick when I'd held him at his baptism and he'd found humor in the minister's wet touch on his forehead.

But on the drive up the Gorge, Nick wasn't even giving us the chance to hope for that laugh, or for much of anything. Carl and I finally quit trying and didn't even say much to one another for the rest of the way to the exit. There was an ache in the car, of the loss we knew was coming, not just of Paul and Dee together, but of us with them, of us with Nick, the way it used to be; and for Nick and all the things he wouldn't say.

#

In the parking lot, next to the trail head, it didn't take long after we got out of the Jeep to pick up the dead fish smell in the air. It was fall and the leaves had mostly turned, orange and yellow and gold, so it should've been the smell of dried leaves and the must of earth that's finally gotten some rain after a hot summer.

No one said anything at first, but the smell didn't go away. I folded three dollar bills into a small enough rectangle to fit in the little envelope, wrote our name and license plate on it and the fact that there were three of us hiking, and put the envelope in the metal slot. "Do you smell that?" I called over to Carl and Nick. They each had a boot up on the bumper of the Jeep, leaned over tying their laces, not talking. "Yeah," said Carl. Nick didn't look up. Thick chunks of his brown hair had fallen forward and I couldn't see his face. He still had the music in his ears.

We left the parking lot and the sound of the water got louder and the smell stronger. The trail ran beside the creek, which was still hidden by trees and undergrowth. By the time we started on the trail, the smell had settled deep in my throat and I had an urge to gag.

Instead, I got up in front of Nick and stopped him by putting both hands on his shoulders. He stepped back and I let go, but not before I felt him there, through his shirt, his shoulders were round and strong and there was the sinew, the fine strings of deltoids under my thumb. After I let go, I mouthed in a big way, "Can you hear me?" Nick rolled his eyes and pulled the ear buds out. "No music on the trail." I was surprised at how clear I said it, without any of the worry that was in me. "You can listen to the sound of the creek, the wind." I said it in the way I used to tell him, on an overnight with Carl and me, that he couldn't have any more ice cream or that it was time to go to bed. "You can listen to Carl make stupid jokes, you can listen to me, or you can ignore us. But enough with the music." Nick rolled his eyes again and jammed the cords into his pocket. That's when I wasn't so sure whether my voice had been clear and calm, or if I'd said enough or too much, or if this was even the right thing we were doing with Nick today.

The trail dipped down and there was a clearing to the creek. The water was low. In some places it was small pools amid big flat rocks. The creek was thick with salmon, live and dead and dying. Most of them had lost the rainbow of their scales and instead had gray and white spots of flesh that looked like it had been torn or bitten. Some of the fish were in the small pools, fanning their tails. Others tried to move up the creek, curling into U's made of heads and tails and then snapping themselves flat and leaping, just a few inches further up. Sometimes they'd get to a place where there was more water but it was flowing against the direction they were headed and it was hard work.

There were so many salmon, that if we'd wanted to we could have walked across the water on dying fish.

We were in a row, next to this place by the creek and I was between Carl and Nick. Nick looked over me, to Carl. "Why are they like that?" Nick's voice had the rough sound that came from a long time of not talking. His voice made all the other sounds drop away, the creek, the wind, the slap of the salmon on rocks, all got quiet when Nick spoke.

Carl said it was spawning season. He said it like Nick had been talking the whole time we'd been together, without any surprise and not too many words. "They're trying to get as far upstream as they can before they lay their eggs and fertilize them, before they die."

I was glad when Nick asked the next question. "But why do they look like that, all torn up?" Because even though I'd grown up in Oregon, had hiked along plenty of creeks and rivers, and had once caught a salmon, I'd never hiked when the spawn was happening. I didn't see how this smell, this ugly flesh, could have anything to do with making life.

"I'm not really sure," Carl turned and started up the trail. "It has something to do with them going from salt to fresh water."

I followed Carl. The trail was still damp from the rain the day before. That, mixed with the pine needles and leaves, made the ground spongy and like the quiet of walking on carpet. I stopped a way on, and looked back. Nick was still standing by the creek. He'd picked up a branch and was poking at one of the fish. Carl stopped too, just in front of me. He put a hand on my shoulder when I opened my mouth to say something to Nick. "Let's go." Carl's voice was just loud enough for me to hear.

Carl and I went around a small bend and up the trail. "You don't have to hover like that." Carl didn't turn when he said it, but I could hear him because the creek had dropped away below us and it was quieter here. And because he'd raised his voice a little, so I'd be sure to hear. "You just have to give him some room to get through this."

How he said this, like he knew better than me what Nick needed, made me mad. But my voice was soft when I said, "I'm not hovering." Soft but with some edge to it, that said Carl was wrong, that we needed to watch Nick, needed to take extra care of him. "I'm just worried about him." I said. "He needs to talk."

"You're the one who needs to talk." Carl pulled a red bandana from his pocket and wiped his forehead with it. "You've done nothing but talk about Paul and Dee since the day they told us." He put the bandana back in his pocket. "It doesn't make any difference."

Even though what he said had some truth in it, I was embarrassed. Apparently I'd been tiring Carl out with all my talk. But it was the way I'd always worked through things, chewing on them with my words. I put my hands on my hips, my head forward a little, to say the next thing.

"Honey." Carl tilted his head to the side, and he said this with a coax to it, a way he had of trying to herd me away from being mad. "I don't want to fight. Nick just needs us to be with him. Can you do that, can you just be with him and not push it?"

Before I agreed to anything, Nick was there, quiet behind us. There was no way to know if he'd heard us or not, but it was like his eyes took a step back. He stopped on the trail and looked from one of us to the other, Carl and I facing each other, me with my hands still on my hips. Maybe that's why, when I said in a big fake voice, "Well look who's here, we were wondering if you were going to join us," I was embarrassed again. Carl turned around and moved on up the trail.

Nick still had the branch in his hand and he used it as a walking stick. He was quiet for awhile and I wasn't sure what he was talking about at first when he said, "I don't see why they have to die and get all messed up like that." Nick swung the stick up just above our heads, at a cobweb that was strung from a tree on one side, to a boulder on the other. "Just to make more fish."

Partly because of what Carl had said, but more because I didn't have the answer, I didn't say anything back to Nick. Just walked along beside him as the quieting of the creek mixed in with the small breeze and with the leaves letting go and ticking down.

Paul and Dee asked us to be Nick's godparents before Nick was even born. We'd been at their house for dinner and Dee told us that Nick had just started to kick. We took turns putting our hands on Dee's stomach and Dee tried to tell us what it was like, to feel him inside her. There was a moment of quiet when she couldn't find the right words, a moment when it was as if we were listening for the drum of his feet against her stomach. In that quiet, she told us about how she and Paul had agreed we were the ones to ask, before any of their brothers or sisters or any of their other friends. Dee said, "We want him to have second parents, the kind he can go to when he can't go to us." I hadn't known what it would mean, how hard it would get to be, how I'd hit a point when I didn't know what to say to him.

The trail took us up in switchbacks for about a mile and a half, then there was a straight and steady rise. We met a few people coming back the other way. There were two young women with a golden lab. Nick squatted down to pet the lab that had gotten ahead of the women. When they came along and apologized about their dog, Nick stood up quick and moved to catch up with us again, his head down and his hair covering his face. When had he gone from being such an open boy, who'd talk to anyone, to this way he was so awkward with pretty women, with strangers, with old friends?

A short way on, Nick called out to us. "Hey." The sound of this was louder than anything he'd said that day; it had more hope in it. "Look what I've got." Carl and I turned back and Nick came toward us, his hands held out in front of him, in a kind of balancing back and forth. A small snake, black with white stripes, dropped from one hand to the other, curling around and trying to slip away. "It's a snake." Nick's eyes were wide and the turning up of his mouth held the old joy that always used to be a part of being with Nick.

We were close enough now that I could reach out too. Nick let the snake drop in my hands, then put his hands under mine to catch it again. Snakes were something I'd never minded much. I always found a strange comfort at the feel of them in my hands, especially these thin ones, garter snakes.

"Can I keep it?" Nick wasn't really asking and he answered before we could say anything. He said, "I'm going to keep it," before I could say all the things that were reasons he couldn't: that you don't take things from the forest, how would he carry it for the rest of the hike, how would he carry it in the Jeep, that Dee wouldn't want him to have a snake in the house and wouldn't take care of it when he went to his dad's place. That the snake would die and be another disappointment to Nick.

Before I could even consider whether I should try to stop Nick, it was Carl who said, "Oh, Nicky." But then Carl noticed my own quiet, maybe read all the words that were in me. He just said, "Yeah," and his voice lifted up and away from what he'd been thinking before. No became yes. "Okay, then. Carl said. He started up the trail again. "We should be getting close to the falls, then we can eat something."

#

At first I wasn't sure if the sound was the falls or not, then it picked up and got louder, the air cooled and there was a dampness to it. The trail opened out to a clearing under the trees, where the water coming from the side of the mountain was loudest. The ground here was bare; a place where people stopped over the years to watch the waterfall, which was up and off to our left. We were midway between where the falls started and where it ended, the place where we could see the white of the water coming down, catch the prism colors in the mist, see the land of the water in the big pool that spread out from white to calm below us.

We were quiet again, in a row like before, Carl and me and Nick. Here the air was clean and smelled of cedar and fir and compost. Nick had taken the snake out of his pocket. He dropped it from hand to hand, like the water in that waterfall.

Carl stepped back and slipped the pack off. "I'm hungry," he said. "Let's see what we've got here." There were no surprises, it was what we always took on a hike: peanut butter and jam sandwiches, cheddar cheese and mayonnaise sandwiches, Frito chips, oatmeal cookies. Carl pulled out five sandwiches, each wrapped in its own Ziploc. They'd flattened in the pack and would be warmed up now, with the cheese soft and the peanut butter and jam melting into each other. I sat down next to Carl and pulled out napkins and water.

"Nick." Carl said.

Nick was still at the ledge, looking out at the falls. He turned around, put the snake back in his pocket, and brushed his hands on his jeans.

Carl held out a sandwich, ready to toss it to Nick. "Here's your PB&J, buddy."

"I don't really like that anymore." Nick came over and squatted down by the pile of sandwiches. "Do you have something else?"

It was in that small thing that I saw how much Carl was hurting in all this, in all the ways things had changed, but especially in the way Nick seemed to have moved away from us, the way we didn't know him so well anymore. Carl just shrugged and said, "Suit yourself."

We were quiet while we ate. The noise of the falls made it hard to talk anyway. We finished up the chips and cookies and all had long drinks of water. Nick and Carl were up, looking at the falls again. I put everything away, then stretched out my legs and rested my head on the backpack. "I could use a snooze."

My eyes weren't closed for more than fifteen seconds when Nick's voice rose up, "Where'd it go?" And it was the sound of him as a little boy, his voice breaking and thin. I sat up and saw Nick moving back and forth over the clearing, looking at the ground, coming to rocks and shrubs, reaching in and under them. Carl started to look too and so did I.

Of course the snake had found its way out, dropped down to the ground and slipped away. It was selfish for me to have the relief, knowing that snake had gone back where it belonged. I'd always hated seeing a thing trapped and I was also glad to let go of the worry about how Nick would take care of it. But the way he was searching, his cheeks flushed red, it was another small hope that had slipped away from him and there was, again, nothing to say to make it right.

Of course I tried. "Oh sweetie," I said. "I'm sorry. I guess that snake just wanted its freedom." It was stupid of me. Carl was right, it was better not to say anything.

Nick yelled at me then. "You don't care." There were tears starting in his eyes and it was easy to see he was mad about that too. "I wanted it. I just wanted that one thing." He went past me then and I reached for him. He pushed me on the shoulder in a way that made me stumble back. "Leave me alone." His voice was deep now, with tears and anger and there was nothing in it that said he knew who I was.

Carl was behind me and he caught me and kept me standing. We watched Nick until he disappeared from the clearing and down the trail.

I turned to Carl then. My own tears had started, but they were tired, tired of trying to find the right thing to say, the words that would fix this thing. Carl put his arms around me and held me there, next to the big sound of the falls, under the trees, some green with needles and some letting go of their leaves, bit by bit.

Carl eased up on his holding and we moved apart. He reached down and picked up the backpack and we left the falls and went after Nick. He wasn't far, just a few minutes down the trail. He was on a rock at the side of the trail, sitting with his knees up and the tears coming now in a quiet way, him using the back of his hands to wipe them away.

There are some things you know, that you don't have to think about. I got up beside Nick on that rock and put both arms all the way around him. I pulled him to me and put his head to my shoulder. I kept him there, even when he first tried to pull away, even after he took a deep breath and the tears came harder for awhile, even when his snot and tears were on my shoulder. I had no words then, just the sounds of holding a child and the feel of Carl beside us.

I didn't let go until Nick said, "I can't breathe." His nose was stuffed up and the words had that sound of long cried tears.

We were all a little shy then and the best thing seemed to be to move, to go down that trail as fast as we could, our feet making a quiet pounding on that soft ground.

The fish and their smell were still there at the end of the trail. Maybe some that were alive when we came through were dead now, and maybe others had moved up a little further and laid their eggs. There was no way to tell and we didn't stop to find out.

On the drive back up along the Columbia we were quiet. The river made white crests on small waves. The light had changed and our side of the river was in shade and everything on the other side was the gold of October.

Six Degrees of Juicy

~

Lynn Veach Sadler

We spent our honeymoon in London. David didn't ask my opinion. Grandmother Jessie said it was the "groom's prerogative" and not to pout. Besides, like me, she "purely loved" his accent. I preferred Hvar Island, the "Croatian Madeira." Not just for its literary/cultural history. To see what I could do about its weather. It boasted of having the most sunshine in Croatia. The hotels give discounts when it's cloudy, free days if there's snow. Eight snowy days in the last ten years! I'm The Weather Tamer. I thrive, personally and professionally, on Juicy Weather. I could see us on a balcony in the rain eating olive-wrapped anchovies and octopus salad, sipping slivovitz, and organizing a rave in the local disco, after which I'd recite all my verses for Hvar. I'd had a grant for a lecture/reading tour in Dubrovnik and had traveled extensively in Croatia. I'd written a book-length collection of poems about the experience. David *couldn't* be ignorant of the source of Saint Euphemia!

To prove I wasn't limp-waisted, I suggested a "flash trip" to Paris. (I'm becoming semi-well-known for flash fiction.) Afterwards, I pronounced the excursion "juicy." David looked at me funny and asked what that "obvious Southernism" meant. Which alarmed me. The "obvious" most of all. While he slept that night, I penned "Paris by Rain" and left it on his bedside table. Even if you were born on the wrong side of the Mason-Dixon Blanket, you can infer that "juicy" means more than rainy.

Paris by Rain

We went to Paris for the day.
To see its sights? *Oui, s'il vous plait*!
Fast train through Chunnel made our way.
It rained and rained and rained and rained.
First came bus ride through Paris streets.
Upon Seine boat we next took seats,
then stormed the Louvre to play aesthetes.
It rained and rained and rained and rained.

Can Paris still be gay in rain?
It was indeed upon the Seine!
We did not want to re-entrain.
It rained and rained and rained and rained.
The gray-brown Seine splashed, leapt, and rang.
The gargoyles gurgled as rain sprang.
Dead walls of Notre Dame tossed tang.
It rained and rained and rained and rained.
All ran into a fine Monet.
The colors blended in nosegay.
We came here for the rain's soirée!
It rained and rained and rained and rained.
The Mona Lisa smiled and smiled.
We looked about for Oscar Wilde,
to London still unreconciled.
It rained and rained and rained and rained.
The lovers dripped but yet entwined.
Their arms grown vines, their kisses brined.
Upon each other's rain they dined.
It rained and rained and rained and rained.

When finally we must leave her,
Sweet Paris had our secret *coeur*,
created us her chorister.
It rained and rained and rained and rained.
And, when upon the London train,
we toasted Paris with champagne,
ate her baguettes, and watched her rain.
She rained and rained and rained and rained.
I didn't tell David it's in the sophisticated form *kyrielle* lest he deem me "overreaching."

I'm Originally-Southern. David *does* assess me as an original. He's from NYC *and* an ad man. Which is why I can be construed as "overreaching." Which is also where we met. On the fiftieth anniversary of *Catcher in the Rye*. I was "in town" to see my agent. I managed to disengage from "Victoria" before having to eat, suavely, the *gritsé-sous-glassé* she'd order for me, grinning like a you-know-what, and went on my secret mission: Central Park. It was raining mightily. Serendipity.

That was how I first came to *fascinate* [his term] David. His pick-up—a "six" [my rating]—involved sidling up to ask, "Pardon me, have you seen a lost Schnauzer?" as he dangled a leash under my nose.

Pure put-on. The leash was new and didn't smell of wet dog. But the "come-on" *was* original, and I carry three stun-pens, courtesy of Grandmother Jessie, whenever I'm in "Parts North." I wasn't worried about being ravished. Besides, also courtesy of Grandmother Jessie, I'm a black, not to say "polka-dotted," belt.

"I've seen no dogs, lost or otherwise, though it's a day for raining you-know-what's." My air was matter-of-fact-with-a-*soupçon*-of-*eau-de-disgust*, but he didn't notice, just stared. A bit off-putting. My hair opts for rigor mortis in the damp, much less flat-down rain. It was standing out a yard from my head. I inherited it from Grandmother-Jessie-aforementioned. It's how she identified me as her genuine heir *from my cradle*.

He just stared down at me. I've always liked tall men with well-hung cabooses.

"I'm sorry about your dog, but I'm not guilty."

"What? Oh, he'll come home alone."

"I've heard that."

"Heard . . . what?"

"That all dogs come home to roost."

He stared, gave a puny laugh that throttled into a snort worthy of Odin. I was hooked.

"Can you tell me why this is a 'lagoon'?"

"*Lagoon?*"

"All the way through Salinger's *Catcher in the Rye*, whose fiftieth anniversary this is, Holden Caulfield worries about where the ducks go in winter when the lagoon freezes over. Why would water in Central Park, NYC, be called a 'lagoon'?"

The sun came out then, and David asked if I'd like to see the rest of the park. We closed our umbrellas, and he put away his leash. We walked and talked, and the world went all-Julia-Roberts-wandering-into-what's-his-name's-bookstore.

Juicier. Thunder and lightning again but at some distance. Then the rain began. The juiciness we were walking-in-a-slow-dance-through gradually darkened.

Hoodlum One and Hoodlum Two suddenly plunge into, shatter our juiciness. One of them—Hoodlum One in my re-plays—puts a knife to my neck. I think of my stun-pens. Too late. Hoodlum Two twists David's arm behind his back, threatens with a larger knife. The storm's noise increases, but that may have been *after*shadowing.

Hoodlum One/Snake addresses David: "Old Father Hubbardbucks and his sweet doggy bone, I and my partner salute you. Bat and me got bones of our own that ain't been delivered yet."

Hoodlum Two/Bat shakes David. "He's ready for it, Snake. Ready and waitin.'"

Snake, well-named, hisses venom. "All Old Father Hubbardbucks's bucks can't keep us away from his sweet doggy bone. We gots a taste for sweet meat."

I've no idea where my "weapon" came from. From being Grandmother Jessie's granddaughter? From wanting to be brave before David? From my head-to-toes belief in the efficacy of literature? From my anger—goddamn-deep-down—that I had incipient juiciness in the flesh, as it were, and these no-nums had the audacity to . . . ?

I ask sweetly, matter-of-factly: "Does your mother know you're out? Does she know you're Lear run mad in storm?"

Predictably, this salvo rattles Bat's cage. "What she mean, Snake?"

Snake's no pushover. (Else he wouldn't be Number One, would he, Jo-Jo?) "Forget it! Crazy-broad talk. Shut up, girl!"

Up pops one of my Croatian poems, "Flesh," about a martyrdom. "Does your mother know you're eating Saint Euphemia's flesh?"

Bright Snake. A quick study. "Shut up, bitch-witch!"

I watch Bat, talk to/at Snake. I, too, am surprised when David joins in. "You're on to her. She's the third witch in *Macbeth*. The one who turns herself into Lady Macbeth."

Bat's apprehensive; he never misses *Buffy the Vampire Slayer*. "Jesus God, Snake! What if that woman's a witch?"

Righteous leader Snake rushes to reassure his underling. "Hang tough, fool! They're bluffin'."

I feed them Saint Euphemia, piece by piece. "Two men to hold me?/Gentle gashes through my softest flesh./They know the flesh,/what hurts most./Our father, bless me./Keep me strong to bear this war on flesh./My flesh is a hill they will climb./Flesh's parts removed,/one by one./A pile: one leg, one arm, a knee cap, two paps—"

David rushes to aid our audience. "—She means breasts. Paps are breasts."

Bat's own too, too solid flesh melts and not from the blessed juiciness that formerly encased David and me. "Make them stop, Snake! I ain't eat no flesh, ain't cut off nothing from nobody!"

I take no captives. "'—an ear . . . .' I lose count in this hubbub. Could you hold it down, Bat? God's noise I can't do anything about. Yours is a different cup of rain. To continue—'When they take me to the lions, a relief./The lions yawn./The lions are full./The Emperor Diocletian gorges his lions/on Christian flesh./Diocletian's war upon my flesh is finished./My torturers climb hills of flesh,/not mine alone./Don't they gorge on flesh?'"

Snake doesn't know what to do, but, what the Hell? Talk is cheap. "Shut the fuck up, woman! I swear I'll kill you!" He smites the air with his knife.

Close enough for a close shave. His franticness makes him clumsy. I'm assuming he meant to miss.

My voice is not so steady, but Snake and Bat are too polite to notice. "Did I die in faith?/Did I die as I was named?/Euphemia stills." My head lolls over Snake's arm.

David is Johnny-on-the-spot. "You fools! You've killed her! Cursed! You're cursed through all eternity!"

I can't speak for David, but I find Snake's response creative. "Rape him, fool! That'll shut his mouth! And if it won't, you know what to fill it with. Rape him, goddamn it!" Apparently, they don't make hoodlums like they used to.

My sympathies are with Bat. "I don't know what to do, Snake! Help me, Jesus, I don't know what to do!"

"Pull his goddamn pants down, you pussy! Fuck him!"

I'm still considering ramifications when Bat tries to pull down David's Dockers with one hand. I pull from possum drive, go biblical, thinking the while, "Will they think I'm jealous? 'We have a little sister,/and she hath no breasts:/what shall we do for our sister/in the day when she shall be spoken for?'"

Bat's right out of you-know-where. "'Course he ain't got no tiddies. Boys ain't got tiddies. That girl *do* be crazy."

I give him tit for tat. "Oh, he has breasts, but God shriveled them when you ate her flesh."

This rejoinder is definitely not soothing to Bat's digestive processes. "I done tole you, I ain't eatin' no flesh."

My own argumentative appetite is rapacious. "You violated his flesh with your words, and God shriveled up his beasts, dried them like mine." Dramatically, I think, I shouldered myself partly from Snake's grip, scooped my breasts with my hands, and thrust them forth as if offering evidence. Did I tell you I'm of diminutive size? Not flat-chested, exactly, but proportioned as to frame. I couldn't act in Albee's *Three Tall Women*.

That's about it for Bat. "I ain't stayin' here, Snake!"

Snake's not yet ripe. "Wait, Bat! It's some kind of trick they're pullin'. They're in cahoots. I can prove it."

David and I are with Bat. "How you gonna prove anything?"

Whatever game of sexual identity we are in has long since lost me, but Snake has it all figured out. "Tear off his goddamn shirt. You'll see. No breasts. He's a male. Tear off the shirt. They's connin' you."

Bat's no longer my favorite. "Let's jest kill 'em and get the hell away from here, Snake!"

Having made my verbal bed, I've no choice but to continue lying from it. "Because she died well,/her flesh—bones?—/what was left—/hardly a *body*—/was carried to Constantinople./Lay there, remembering, long centuries./Then she willed it gone./Was she not sufficiently a martyr?/She was saint ere this new moving of the 'flesh.'"

Dear Bat wants nothing so much as to bring both hands to his ears, but he doesn't dare let the one with the knife move from David's throat. He starts to pull it away, wavers, doesn't know what to do. "I'm goin' crazy! Stop her voice!"

I don't think it's *that* bad. David doesn't seem to mind, and he's a Yankee, too.

"Shut her up, Snake!"

Maybe if he'd say please, but he doesn't. I continue. "Saint Euphemia's sarcophagus appeared off Rovinj in a spectral boat."

David plays Boswell to my Dr. Johnson. "'Spectral' is ghost. I warned you, but you wouldn't listen. Now the Ghost Boat's coming after you!"

I swear, by all Bat holds holy, I make the rest up right there, roaring along on the current in David's Ghost Boat. Maybe all the talk of breasts gave me the cows. "We could not move that spectral boat,/though we knew it Saint Euphemia's./We sat upon the sand and waited./Young Iginio came./Behind him, two spectral cows,/cows that were flesh no more,/had they ever been./At the boy Iginio's nod,/the two cows knelt and lifted/with bowed heads/Saint Euphemia's sarcophagus/from sea and sand./The seaweed fell away/and worshiped,/rose up to stand on end./Worshiping, too, were all the people of Rovinj."

David hops aboard. "It rained, rained, rained in revenge! It rained like today. Like now! You two've made it come again!

Snake remains determined. "Bring him here to me! Then you cover the girl."

Bat half-drags David to Snake. They exchange us. I continue to work them with my rain of words. "That night, all of Rovinj helped the sacred cows/drag Saint Euphemia's sarcophagus/to the top of Rovinj's hill./We could see our working hands/through the blue-lit bodies of the smiling cows./We placed our burden in/the tiny Church of

Saint George./The two cows floated out."

Snake's ignoring me. He thrusts David before him, knife tip at his throat. "Undress. *Now!*"

I'm peremptory. "Hey, Snake, something I said?"

All three males ignore me. So? They'll need more to trip me.

Slowly, gracefully, teasingly, as if strip-dancing, David pulls off his Burberry, tie . . . pulls out the shirt, begins unbuttoning . . . . Snake grabs the collar. His knife spits buttons. "Open it." Now who's sweet and matter-of-fact?

I can't resist. "Excuse me, you two, you're gay? I know your blades are. Does it therefore follow—?"

David pulls Poor Shirt open. I'm craning with Snake and Bat. I ponder: David being Jewish, wouldn't it have been more interesting to have him bare his nether parts? I spy a mat of black-black hair. I can't see his breast buds, but I'm a bit nearsighted.

Suddenly, distant sirens, nearing whistles. Our friends flee.

We needed closure; I rallied, found safety pins for David's shirt, recited while he re-dressed. "Later we built, where a church had been,/The Cathedral of Saint Euphemia,/the largest such—*baroque* they call it—/in all Istria./We have a relief in purest marble/of Saint Euphemia./We have her tomb behind the altar on the right./Her bell tower was modeled after the Venetians' St. Mark's./It is the tallest in all Istria./Saint Euphemia stands upon it,/her flesh returned in copper/from the rain./She is Rovinj's weather vane."

I'm glad the cops didn't nab Snake and Bat; they were outraged enough by our shorthand version. Think how Our Resident Hoodlums would have inflated the episode.

When we left the station where they'd "filed the report," we had dinner. No rain, but everything got juicier anyhow.

I hit David while he was reeling. "Salinger was apropos."

He started. "Because I'm Jewish?"

"No. The gangster tie-in." I was probably a bit smug.

"Salinger was tied to gangsters?"

"No. Do you watch *The Sopranos*?"

The fact that he'd seen part of one episode was his first chink. But he hadn't hidden his ignorance. That was good, wasn't it?

"Tony, the star, is always worrying about the ducks flying away from his pool and where they go in winter. He lives in New Jersey, but that's only a sirenful from Central Park. Holden Caulfield maybe grew into Tony Soprano."

Silence. I refused to cover it. David wasn't the tiniest bit embarrassed. That was good, too, wasn't it?

"Is this, like, a Jimmy Hoffa thing with you?"

I laughed. "Heavens-no. You may not know how many *real* criminals have adored Salinger's antihero. Holden. A lot of them are listed in John Guare's play, *Six Degrees of Separation*."

I watched delightedly as David brought out, then scribbled in his Day Planner.

"Six *what*?"

"*Degrees of Separation*. John G-u-a-r-e. It antedated the Mel Gibson conspiracy movie. He was always buying a copy of *Catcher*, but he was a good guy."

"Not a *made* one."

We both laughed. Great line. That was very-*very*-good, wasn't it?

David wrote in my name and appurtenances, too. We exchanged cards, but he still entered my vitals. Very-very-*very*-good.

"One thing I still don't know."

If he was that self-confident, I wasn't going to lick the red off his history. "What?"

"Why you're obsessed with rain."

"I'd quibble with *obsessed*. Grandmother Jessie bequeathed the rain-thing."

I'd have been sad-plus if he'd nodded and let it go.

"You want to unpack or leave me on the Central Park beach, a fish on the sand gulping for air?"

I liked the man's words and images.

He wasn't the first to notice my love affair with rain, if not with juicy weather per se.

"If you decide you've had enough, point a finger skyward. If you're really tired, use your index finger."

His mouth crumpled around the edges; he sputtered. "Deal."

"When I turned teenager, Grandmother Jessie asked, 'How intelligent do you think chimpanzees are, Jo-Jo?'"

"'I've seen the stuff by that Goodall broad on TV. She thinks they're hot shit.' I couldn't use words like that around Mother."

"What do *you* think?"

"Hey, Old Woman, I'm a kid. Why do you want my opinion on *anything*?"

"You claim the Fifth of Kid when it suits."

"Yeah. Let's have Lecture 5,083."

"That's how Grandmother Jessie and I relate. 'Banter,' 'giving as good as you get,' she calls it. I love it. Love *her*."

David seems interested, gives visual reinforcements.

"Grandmother Jessie was right on about rain games standing me in good stead. To wit."

"Don't let anybody, Ms. Goodall included, Jo-Jo, put you on about chimpanzees. They're cute and surface bright, but they sit under trees with their heads down when it rains and wait until it's over."

"I considered. 'That sounds pretty smart.'"

"I wouldn't say so, Jo-Jo. That makes the rain down time."

"Chimpanzees have to live, too."

"Choices, Jo-Jo. Chimpanzees wait out the rain, getting nowhere. Or?"

"Or what?"

"You tell me."

"I gave my standard Groan-for-Grandmother-Jessie. 'Another lesson for the kid. I should of—should *have* known.'"

"Immaterial, Sweet-Young-Jo-Jo."

"They say you're crazy."

"And chimpanzees fly. Jo-Jo, you're such a kid. If you're going to play in *my* game preserve, I'll thank you to be specific. *Who* said? You mean your mother."

"And you're such an adult, you had to teach with chimpanzees. What?"

"What *what*?"

"What lesson? I'm all ears."

"As an adolescent, you're all body parts, but I seriously doubt that ears are among them."

"Should you talk to me like that?"

"I think it's just how you should be talked to. I thought you had some insight."

"Insight into—?"

"Chimpanzees. No slight intended. To *either* creature. Are chimpanzees dumb enough to spend three-quarters of their lives waiting out rain?"

"You want me to say, 'No, Grandmother Jessie, chimpanzees use Raintime for thinking.'"

"Give that Sweet-Young-Thing a golden banana! And what's the weather doing today, Jo-Jo?"

"Raining."

"And what will I do?"

"Think!"

"Give that Sweet-Young-Thing a golden-banana-cut-on-the-bias."

"I'm not welcome when it's raining?"

"I've nothing against double-think, Jo-Jo. Only doublespeak. I don't mean Orwellian doublethink. It's spelled as one word. D-o-u-b-l-e-t-h-i-n-k. I mean two brains thinking. D-o-u-b-l-e-HYPHEN-t-h-i-n-k."

"You refer to Orwell. *1984.*"

"The lass thinks before she has to. I was right about her."

"I'll admit most grown-ups talk as if we weren't present, but you raise it to an art form."

"It's your call."

"I wouldn't miss it."

"I didn't derive *thinking* chimpanzees from the world's Jane Goodalls . . . *or* from Tarzan or Clint Eastwood but from experience. Your Dead Grandfather Les—at least I think he finally persuaded me to marry him—and I were on this big flamingo lake in Kenya—what *was* its name? I climbed a rise and sat down on a log to watch the wildlife and think how lucky I was to be there. A chimpanzee came up and sat on a log close by. He assumed the thinking pose, too."

"Rodin's."

"Grandmother Jessie gave one of her all-approving nods. 'Good girl. Les took our picture. Won a contest in *Parade Magazine.* He called it *The Thinker(s). S* in parentheses. I don't know if the chimpanzee was imitating me or doing his own thing. I *choose* to think the latter. I *choose* to think he was puzzling about why he evolved into us, why we and not chimpanzees and other apes came to be preferred.'"

"Maybe he was just coming on to you."

"Thanks for the kindest comment any human's made about me in years."

"He had King-Kong Syndrome. I like Fay Wray better, but you look like Jessica Lange. You may be old, but you're not bad-looking. Your figure's quite good. But you do work out. It's another thing Mother hates."

"Precisely why I do it, my girl. It's for my son's wife's benefit when you see me before my giant-screened television set working out with the likes of Jane Fonda, Suzanne Sommers, Gloria Swanson. . . . Did I tell you about the time the Wild Man of Borneo—?"

"That's Grandmother Jessie in an earful, David."

My ad man was summative. "Since then, you've worked in rain."

"Something like that" was my response, but he'd made Grandmother Jessie's gift to me much too plebeian and hadn't pursued her Wild Man of Borneo.

Nonetheless, before I hardly knew where to scratch my bite,

we were being married. Had the term *juicy's* pretty head reared at him before the honeymoon, I'd not have rushed headlong. Besides, the families objected, which very much helped. My only pause was for Grandmother Jessie's gentle, "Can The-Poet-Laureate-of-Barbecue find happiness with The-Jewish-Prince-of-New-York-City-No-Matter-How-Beautiful?" She referred to my having had "The Land of *Pork*ahontas," a comic-epic "poem" nominating whole-hog barbecue as North Carolina's state food, published in Massachusetts' *Tips from the Pit*, which had designated me "*Pork* Laureate." I considered, then shrugged. If culinary differences were irreconcilable, there'd always be trips "home" and orders flown up from Pig Man. If Elizabeth Taylor could have chili follow her around the world, surely I could get my particular Southern Comfort via internet. I was already comforted by her having married somebody Jewish.

Thus I found myself hearing David dismiss "our" honeymoon's Paris poem with "So juicy means rainy." He had the grace to halt quarter-shrug.

Juicy isn't just rain and dampness but impure and adulterated steaminess. If you can't stand The Long Hot Summer, never put foot in The Southern Kitchen. Much less its bedroom. Juicy is sibilant-silk, sheet-knotting, hairy-chested, hot-hot-hot-sticky-wicked-wet, cat-on-a-hot-tin-roof, The-Young-Elizabeth-Taylor-in-teddy-and-buck-"nekked"-bottom WEATHER/LOVE/LIFE.

Grandmother Jessie wanted to take out a contract on the man who wrote the song about that woman letting her hair hang down because it would alert the Yankees to the real Southern treasure trove. But it was country-western; the Yankees didn't hear it, much less tumble. All that crap about Southern women with granny gowns and forty layers of bedding pulled to the neck and nailed down all around them is just that. Southern women come with surprises for *deserving* men. I was biding our time to give mine fully to David. The time increased when he fumbled over *juicy*.

We flew to Heathrow and were returning on the final leg of Holland America's World Cruise on the *Rotterdam*. I was fairly sure my marriage wasn't going to work out by that time and considered flying home for an annulment or whatever was permitted a Jewish-Southern union, but Grandmother Jessie's return e-mail had cautioned forbearance. She also reminded me that the weather could go "quite juicy" crossing the North Atlantic.

As usual, Grandmother Jessie was right. I tried to hide my elation, but anyone noticing me would have assumed that my rosy cheeks, sparkling eyes, and general bonhomie bespoke connubial satisfaction. Wrong. David was as seasick as the rest of the passengers and didn't approach the dining room again after we'd seen people tipping over in their chairs.

The evening shows went on, happily, and I was pleased to have them. I holed up in our cabin at my laptop all day writing, punctuated with deck (when we were allowed outside) or corridor walks. I also fetched whatever David thought might soothe his troubled innards, e.g., apples, crackers, plain oatmeal.

The first night David could again venture out, the entertainer was a Jewish singer born in Israel but living in Florida. She was a crowd-pleaser, a regular on the World Cruise. She ended her performance with "Let There Be Peace on Earth" (". . . and let it begin with me"). Everybody except the codgers asleep in the front rows was crying. Tears are right up there with rain in my book anyhow.

The next morning, David was restless from all the inactivity, so we went to the Java Bar. As I lapped my latté and he sipped a plain coffee, we realized that, at the table next to us, was last evening's performer talking away to a couple we'd met. We hadn't noticed her because she wasn't wearing makeup and was in jeans. We immediately recognized her ringing voice, though. What she said conveyed that it had been said many times before. I'm sure I don't have it word-for-word, but most of it is here.

"An Arab is an Arab is an Arab. A little desert man. They let him out with oil. And now because of oil, he sits among the leaders of the world making decisions for the world. Well, he can't make decisions for Israel. Keep him in the desert. He's a Bedouin. A little desert man. One of these days, Israel will get tired of it all again and bomb the shit out of those little desert men, say to the world, 'World, what do you think of that?' I'm not religious, but I know the Bible for its history. The Bible says, 'Trouble will come out of the North.' It means the little desert men. They took what they wanted from the Old Testament. Yes, their language is Semitic. But Jews and Arabs never will be friends! Their cultures are different. You can't change a person's culture. We have to accept that Jews and Arabs never will be friends and get on with the world. America says it won the war with the desert man Sadam. Bush counted all the way, proclaimed the Hundred Days' War, said he'd won. Hell, all he did was bomb. And mostly his bombs went wrong. Sadam and his high-and-mighty brought in piles of little desert men, little desert farmers, stacked them in the trenches. Sadam and his high-and-mighty burrowed deep as Hell. They had their gas, but that was all. Their gas and oil. He would have bombed Israel, but all he had was gas. When he attached it to the bombs, they were too heavy, couldn't reach to Israel. I won't watch goddamn CNN! All it does on Israel is the Gaza Strip and Golan Heights! There're hot spots all over the world. In goddamn America, more people are killed in a day by robbers and murderers than in a year in Israel. The whole world's going to be run by murderers and thugs. The little desert men buy them with oil. Only fools watch goddamn CNN! Now Colin Powell plans to provoke to finish the job Old Bush started for New Bush—but mainly for Colin Powell. We need a Burning Bush, but New Bush can 'Burn, Bush, Burn!' He'll be a *small b* burning Bush at most. Any *big B* Burning Bush will come from Israel."

Throughout her litany, I couldn't *not* look at David. His face peacock-tailed the coat of many colors, then went out. Pale and pasty. Then stormy anger. A flash of tears. He wouldn't look at me but didn't resist when I put my hands on his clenched ones there on our table between our cups. I concentrated on unclenching them and on the woman's words. My hands flew up when he suddenly stood, sending his chair falling with a thunderclap. She looked our way, saw him coming. I peeped around his back to watch her face.

He stopped short of her table, folded his arms across his chest, resting his palms on his arms. I could see the live fingers stiff and out as if they wanted to wave at me. His voice was measured. "Woman, I'm Jewish, too. You help no one's cause. The rain falls on Arabs and Jews alike. They both suffer from aridity. It kills the spirit. We all need more rain."

The woman thought David crazy or disloyal, doubtless. At most, he checked her thoughtlessness for some small space of time.

But on me, his wife for thenceforth and forevermore, David's words were a warm rain of rose and orange-blossom water giving off frankincense fumes that perfumed my hair. We went hand-in-hand toward our cabin through a juicy twilight of our own creation. We walked-in-a-slow-dance toward the land of imams and sultans where I would reveal to David the nth degree of a Southern woman's love-making.

Wolf

Donna Trump

It is Sunday, and admission to the Prado Museum is free. My daughter, Gabriella, has bought churros from the vendor down the street. They are warm, and smell of cinnamon. I see grease stains on the paper in which they were wrapped, if only in memory. We have had our coffee. Now that we are ready to go, Gabriella insists on the cane. What use is it when you are with me? I ask. Papa, she says, use the cane. Practice makes perfect. Quizas, I think, but it is not so easy to teach an old man a new thing. She clucks in disapproval as I shrug into an overcoat. It is too warm for a coat, she says.

The walk along the Calle de Felipe IV is short, and the streets are not yet crowded. I feel the presence of the old couples strolling, shadows of two, linked arm in arm. Cars wait patiently as they cross the street to the plaza, where they may sit for a while in the sun. Use the cane, Papa, my daughter reminds me. Move it back and forth in front of you as we walk. I do as she says, my left hand resting lightly on her bent elbow, right hand sweeping the street with the cane.

We approach the museum. Although it is October the smell of roses rests in the warm air. My armpits and back are damp with sweat. People have gathered on and near the stairs to the entrance, and my daughter pulls me close. I pick up the cane, let myself be moved along by the crowd. I hear children, their energy close and big in the small space around me. There is a boy of ten or twelve, I can tell by his smell, by the high pitched, rapid-fire spew of his slang and profanity. I am glad he is here.

At the security check they ask me to put my cane and coat through the scanner, and I am suddenly tired. Then we are in the lobby, a high, domed space cool with stone, voices returning to the center. Where would you like to go today? Gabriella asks. A joke, of course. It is always Velasquez and Goya. Her favorite and mine, for as long as we have come. She sighs, a little too loudly, as she assists me back into the coat.

We have changed places, as quickly and deceptively as cards in a magician's hand. I used to position her in front of me, encourage her to walk right up to the huge canvasses, close enough to see the brush strokes. What do you see? I would ask. It is like a photograph, she would say, mesmerized by the dresses, the fair hair and skin of a girl in *Las Meninas*, the sparkling thorns sticking into and out of Jesus' head in *The Crucifixion.* I prepared for the day she would refuse to come, too busy, ashamed of being seen with her father. It never arrived, but this one has: the day where I stand in front of her, her hand at the small of my back. What do you see, Papa? she asks.

I see Goya's dark paintings best, the ones he painted late in life when he was deaf, and perhaps mad. There is Saturn devouring his son, bloody neck and stumps where the head and arms have been bitten off. There are the Fates, suspended above dark ground, lower legs appearing to have been amputated. One Fate holds a scissor with which to cut the string of life, another holds a puppet, grotesquely imagined, devoid of human features.

In front of the painting, I take the cane in one hand, and slip it inside the overcoat. It is not necessary for others to wonder why a blind man covets Goya.

When I was a child, my father took me to the Palacio de Oriente to see the exhibit of Stradivarius stringed instruments. The quartet—two violins, a viola and a cello-- are all of a piece, inlaid at the edges with a geometric pattern of tiny, alternating white and black tiles. There is another Stradivarius in the group, an unadorned cello. This fifth instrument makes the King of Spain's the largest collection of Stradivarius strings in the world, but it is a poor cousin to the other four.

My father was a laborer by trade, a musician at heart. Before the war, he played the cello. Like many other Spanish children, he was removed from his family and Madrid while the civil war waged in the late thirties. When my father returned to Madrid, still a boy of seventeen, his cello was gone—lost, or stolen, or sold—perhaps burned for firewood. His own father had been killed in the war. He joined the only sanctioned trade union of the new regime, El Sindico Vertical, and worked to rebuild Spain. He met my mother shortly thereafter. I was their only child.

I remember their music. Every Sunday, after a breakfast of coffee, breads and pastries, he and my mother would sit in the living room, perched at the edge of mismatched armchairs, and play. My mother held the violin with her chin and strong right hand, fingers trembling in vibrato. My father sat with his back as straight as a needle, knees grazing his new cello, shoulders falling into the bow as he guided and drew it back across the strings. Once a month, my uncles joined them, and the music of the quartet brought each of them, each time, to tears.

We had a small apartment, without the courtyard my mother would have liked. The living area opened up, through two ceiling-to-floor, narrow doors of glass, to a terra cotta tiled balcony, barely one tile wide. I can still see how the notes pushed the glass doors out toward the street, wispy, sheer curtains in their wake. The music floated over the wrought iron balustrade edging the balcony, into the warmth of the early afternoon. I was expected to sit patiently, listening, but I recall little more than the escape of the notes through the open doors, and how I wished I could follow them.

He was not a stupid man, my father. When we visited the Palacio, there was always time for the armor collection as well as the quartet. I was fascinated with all things knighted and medieval, and he was a man who understood passion. He walked slowly through the display, hands clasped at the small of his back, head canted toward me, listening to my tales of chivalry and courage. I would like to say I returned him the favor, paid my respects to the Stradivarius instruments, allowed him the pleasure of meandering through the collection to satisfy his heart. But I was an impatient, fidgety child, and we often left just moments after he passed the last of the four display cases, his hand resting lightly on the glass, fingers splayed.

One afternoon he returned home from work, bottle of red wine in hand. My mother greeted him in the dark portal that passed as a foyer, where they kissed, her palms cradling the sides of his face, his free hand migrating to the back of her skirt, pulling her close. He called us both to the kitchen table, where my mother had set three small glasses. After pouring the wine, he placed the bottle on the marred, cigarette-burned table top, and lifted the tumbler to the two of us.

"I have heard a rumor, my dear Magda," he said, facing my mother, "that the Royal Family is once again holding auditions to play the Stradivarius strings."

It is said a Stradivarius instrument must be played to maintain its beautiful sound. To an observer like me, this is an attractive, even sensual idea, serving up metaphor for all the practiced and unpracticed deeds in a man's life. I suspect my father would have found such popular notions intriguing, but insubstantial. I remember reprinted articles stacked on the cluttered surface of his desk, side by side with folders of sheet music. The reprints were miniature physics lessons, highlighted with graphs of harmonics and frequencies, modified sine waves and vertical hash marks on horizontal lines, dense and tall, short and spaced wide. I took interest in none of it but his talk about the 'wolf' in the Stradivarius cello he longed to play.

"Magda," he said, "Suppose we were to win. How can we be expected to perform with only hours of practice on the King's instruments? We are merely amateurs. The wolf-notes in the cello are notorious."

"David, you are a fine player. Others of our skill have performed. In thirty minutes," she said, "you will have coaxed the wolf out, and tamed it."

"Stradivarius himself would need longer than that, my dear. If you hear the groans, promise me you will play louder, or perhaps faint to distract everyone's attention?"

"Can't you imagine," she said, "that even the wolf will be beautiful?"

When I asked him, later, to tell me about the wolf, he smiled, opened his eyes wide in mock terror, and said, "A wolf, Raul, is a dark creature with sharp claws that will steal a man and devour him in the dead of night." Papa, I protested. But he would only take his heavy, muscled hand and lay it on my head, an uncommon gesture which I loved, and the moment passed.

Two days later, a slab of concrete weighting nearly 500 kilograms slipped out of position at my father's construction site, killing two workers and injuring him and several others. The right side my father's skull was fractured in three places. The bones from his right elbow to the tips of his fingers were crushed beyond repair; it was only a matter of finishing the amputation at the hospital.

My daughter tells me we must leave the museum. She has work to do at home. I would like to offer to help, distract the children, perhaps, but they are teenagers and not much in need of anyone's attention. It is always my hope that one of them will wish to come to the museum with us. Isabel has an unaccountable streak of piety, and prefers Mass on Sunday mornings. Roberto will be in bed well past noon, his mother rousing him on her return. I do not understand why he is allowed to sleep. It is perfectly clear to me I have failed them all, my daughter unable to maintain her marriage, my grandchildren wasting the precious, sighted hours they have on this earth. We leave the Prado in silence.

Traffic has picked up in the early afternoon. As I stand on the corner, automobiles whip by so rapidly my heavy coat is lifted at the hem. There is the impatient idle of engines, the gunning starts, the crescendo and decrescendo of cars speeding along, unstopping. What good this fragile cane is at this juncture, I do not know. Nonetheless, I take a half-step away from the crowd and extend the cane in front of me, a white flag of surrender. I focus on the contrast between light and dark, moving and still, but my heart is in my mouth as I cross the street.

"That was excellent, Papa," Gabriella says. If I were to answer, I would hear my voice shake in fear and infirmity. I nod my head, and offer her my elbow until we reach my flat. "Would you like me to come up?" she asks. Of course I would. The afternoon will be long without her company. Go home, I tell her. I will be fine. I kiss her, tell her she is a good daughter, and turn into the building. The door closes behind me with a rushing out of air, and it is dark.

The surgical amputation of my father's arm crept higher, racing against infection, over the course of the first few weeks. I was not taken to visit him at the hospital, where he languished for months, and so the overheard conversation in which I learned the extent of his disability is seared in my memory, like a brand in the hide of a bull. My mother sat in the living room, holding nothing in her hands but her own face, skin pushed up and back into her dark hair, palms pressed against her cheeks. I saw her in profile only, as I sat at the kitchen table, drawing. She spoke to one of my father's brothers, my Tio Miguel, the viola player in the quartet.

"Have you seen him today, Miguel? Have you seen him?" she demanded.

"Magda, try to calm down. What is it? Has he taken a turn for the worse?"

She laughed, a sound I can still hear, glass dropped on a stone floor. "I think there are no more turns to take." She had come early to the hospital, to discuss my father's progress with his doctor. There is some good news, the physician said. Your husband is up, walking around. His balance is good. But there are concerns about cognition. He appears to have what is called global aphasia—the inability to understand or communicate with language. But you are wrong, my mother said, with confidence. He understands me, she said. I know he understands *me*. I say, come sit next to me, David, and he comes to my side. I say, let me help you with your exercises, and we go through the routine. There is comprehension in his gaze, Doctor, she said. It is true, he speaks gibberish, but I *know* he understands. Me.

I believe he is in therapy right now, Senora Ruiz, the doctor told her. Perhaps we might observe him, together.

I watched from the kitchen as my mother stood up from the chair, a room away. Her hands came together at the center of her face, clasped as if in prayer, extended fingers resting on the bridge of her nose. Then she dropped them, a study in defenselessness. "I showed the doctor everything, Miguel. How David could do whatever I asked of him," she said. "And then the doctor said, 'Only words, Senora. Sit on your hands, and tell your husband what you want him to do.'"

My mother spoke to my uncle as if she wished to kill him, voice inspired by an unearthly possession. "David looked at me, and smiled, with eyes more vacant than those of an infant. He had no idea what I was saying, perhaps no idea who I was. It was the smile, Miguel. Do you know what it's like to see the face of someone you love, inhabited by a stranger?" I remained in the kitchen, the drawing hardly more than a few lines on the page.

Finally, he came home. He was thinner than I remembered, and asymmetrical, shoulders a scale out of balance. My mother sat next to him on the couch, gently stretching the shortened muscles of his left hand. When a person has an injury to one side of his brain, my mother explained, the opposite side of the body suffers. This is why your father's left arm is weak. His left leg was affected, too, she said, but much of its strength has returned. And so it was. My father could get around fairly well, up and down stairs, in and out of a bathroom, or a place at the kitchen table. In his left arm, he had only gross, uncoordinated motion at the shoulder and elbow; use of his left hand never returned. His right arm, which escaped paralysis, was a three inch stump extending from the shoulder. He needed help for everything: eating, dressing, toileting, bathing. It was my job to take care of him after school, while my mother taught the studio of violin students she had assembled. I was ten years old when we started, 14 when he died. This was when I learned patience, and, looking back, how to draw light, and dark, and shadow.

In my apartment, I am almost a sighted man, familiarity with my surroundings lighting up the dark spaces. I turn on the radio. Pachelbel's Canon is just starting. I recognize it immediately from the first four dramatic notes on the cello: high, low, high, low, sustained and majestic. I can see my father playing, rosin shearing off the bow into tiny sprays of glistening white on the shiny, red-brown wood of the cello. The plum colored veins on the backs of his hands are prominent with effort. His body sways, he grimaces and furrows his brow. The other instruments join him, violins and viola each with their own variation of the eight note theme, more themes added and varied into a multi-layered whole. When it is over, I walk to the window and spread open the drapes, and the room lightens, if only a few degrees.

It was my mother who told me about the wolf tones. "The strings vibrate at a certain frequency. You understand that, don't you,

Raul?" she asked. "Well, the whole instrument—sound box, fingerboard, bridge—there is also a very specific frequency at which it vibrates. A wolf note seems to occur," she said, "although no one claims to fully understand it, when the vibrating frequency of the instrument itself equals, exactly, the vibrating frequency of the note being played."

You would think the note might amplify beautifully, or perhaps diminish to zero. But this is not, I have learned, the case. What happens is the instrument is unable to manage the heightened vibration caused by the coincidence of the two frequencies and still create one tone. So it skips from the one note to a harmonic, or series of harmonics. It breaks up the tone into more manageable pieces, but, inexplicably, the notes produced are loud, and harsh, and unpredictable.

My father was the perfect companion for a pre-adolescent boy: bored, non-conversant, and absolutely without judgment. In truth, he was not entirely silent. On his return from the hospital, he often attempted to speak. He had no difficulty forming or saying words, but they spilled out of his mouth in such a cascade of nonsense even he appeared to be frightened by their anarchy. Within months, the futility seemed to overwhelm him, and he closed down the show.

Every day, I came home from school and woke him from his regimented nap, and we hit the streets of Madrid. We walked everywhere, from the Prado to the Palacio de Oriente, the Casa del Campo to the Parque de Retiro, the Plaza Mayor and Puerta del Sol in the heart of the old city to the train stations, north and south. The goal was the simple passage of time. We were always home by dark. If I had schoolwork to do, I did it then, my father sitting at the opposite side of the kitchen table, his eyes fixed on me, expectantly, a passive air of contentment about him. After a hurried job on all the other assignments, I took out my drawing tablet and sketched for him sights from our afternoon adventure: the stolen item from a vendor in the street, the mangy, three-legged dog we discovered in the woods, a stone wall walked, like a tight rope, by a boy and a man with one arm. I drew hastily, hash marks and line, black on white.

When my mother's last student left at nine, we ate dinner. I fed my father piece by piece, bread or cheese or olives. Later in the evening, my mother often played her violin for him, as if the notes might reach what words could not. I would have been happy had it gone on that way, forever. But my father grew more impatient and agitated with the passage of time. The night he rocked uncontrollably, moaning, the arc of movement of his trunk---forward, back, forward, back-- more violent with each line of my mother's music, was the last night I recall her playing for him. After calming him down and getting him to bed, she came out to me, eyes shining. "Your father is frustrated, Raul. This is progress." Tireless in her advocacy for him, she was certain of the next step: we would get him an artificial arm, and allow him the independence and dignity which were his due.

The phone rings in the apartment, and I answer it. "Are you alright, Papa? You seemed tired today, at the museum." It is Gabriella, and I assure her I am fine, but not too quickly, as I want to keep her on the phone.

"What do you hear from your mother, Gaby?" I ask.

"She is well, traveling somewhere, in the States, I believe."

"Is she with that American?"

"Ay, Dios mio, Papa! She is *married* to that American! What do you expect?"

What I expect is that marriages will last, through difficult times: six months after Gabriella was born, November, cold, rain coming down so hard my clothes were soaked by the time I walked the few blocks from the hospital to our apartment in that far away city. Hours past dinner, months since the last break in my studies, I opened the door with numb fingers, made out her shadow, and the shadow of a suitcase, in the dark room. Gabriella's mother sat erect, dressed in her coat and hat. Gabriella was in her arms, wrapped in two or three blankets, making little sucking sounds in her sleep. The baby smelled of milk and the soap used to wash her clothes. I rubbed my nose on my daughter's velvet cheek, wanted to close my eyes but did not dare.

Someone is yelling, harsh and abrupt. *"Papa, are you there?"*

"Yes, yes, of course, Gabriella. Of course your mother is with her husband. I hope they go with God. Speaking of which, how is my Isabel? Is she there? Put her on the line."

By the time I speak with Isabel and Roberto, both conversations abbreviated and strained, I have little left to say. I ask for their mother. "You are a good daughter, Gabriella."

"Ay, Papa, if only it were true. I will see you on Wednesday. Have your grocery list ready. Hasta luego."

"Gabriella?"

"Yes, Papa. What is it?"

"Tell the children I will buy them ice cream if they come along."

"I think a better bet might be Starbuck's."

"Starbuck's?" Ah, yes, Starbuck's, pretty coffee served in monstrous quantity in throw-away containers. "Tell them I will buy them Starbuck's."

I lost him, on more than one occasion, but only once were we found out. It was a dark afternoon, and I was too awash in energy to entertain him inside the flat. We ran through heavy rain to the Metro station at Puerta del Sol, water splashing from the puddles all the way up to my shirt. My laugh echoed in the tunnels of the subway. I continued racing down the steps, the thickening muscles in my legs barely teased by the few blocks we had sprinted. I thought my father was right at my heels. A train straddled the tracks, doors gaping. I jumped in. The doors closed, and the train took off. My father was nowhere to be seen.

I had no choice but to wait until the next station, switch trains and attempt to retrace our steps. Fifteen or twenty minutes had passed. I searched the platform, ran up and down stairs to all the connecting trains. It occurred to me he could be anywhere, but even then, I was not frightened. Once, I got drawn into a soccer game at the park and he grew tired of watching. I found him, an hour later, sitting on the grayed, limestone steps leading into our apartment building. Another time, I lost him briefly in a crowd near the Plaza de Oriente and negotiated his return from an older couple who treated us both to orange juice at a sidewalk café. I was a thirteen, almost fourteen year old boy, waking up every morning feeling bigger, stronger, more alive than I had the day before: I was not worried. No harm would come to my father.

Two hours passed, dusk and bad weather shrouding all of our usual haunts, and we were expected home. Still, I refused to admit error. I came home alone. My mother, bookkeeping at her desk between lessons, looked up at me.

"Where is your father?"

"He's not here?"

"Where is your father, Raul?"

"He'll show up."

She had the apartment searched in minutes, the building in a quarter of an hour. She called the police. They spotted him in a section of the Metro closed off for repair, sitting on the ground with his back against the curve of the underground corridor, weeping. Standing in the foyer, alongside the officer, he reeked of urine, and I saw he had chewed his left arm raw at the wrist. In his eyes there was still panic, and I went to bed, ashamed.

The artificial arm which my mother finally obtained for my father was nothing like the lifelike, computer assisted prosthetic hands of recent years. I remember canvas straps, skinny tubes of fleshy-pink plastic articulated at a metal hinge of an elbow, and of course, the metal claw. I cannot imagine what mountains she must have moved to procure such an expensive, complicated device. It likely was made for someone else.

She worked with him every day for months, but he could not accomplish the complicated sequence of residual arm, shoulder and upper back motions necessary to create movement at the arm's elbow or hook. Years later, in rehabilitation clinics, I observed amputees using these prostheses well, but only with many hours of therapy, determination, and concentrated practice.

"Do you find it amusing, Raul?" she said that evening, eyes fixed on the book on her lap, although I had not seen her turn a page since we sat down after dinner. My father, frustrated and edgy all day, was already in bed for the night in the other room. It was too warm in the apartment, and too small.

I glanced behind me, thinking I had missed something. "Find what amusing?"

She looked up. For the first time, I saw lines in her forehead, the sag of skin at her jaw line. "Letting your father wear the arm slung around his neck, like a necklace."

I didn't think she had seen. "Mama, I don't think he can learn it."

"You don't have the patience to help him, you mean."

"No, I mean I think you should give it up. He doesn't even understand what the arm is for. It may as well be a necklace, or a noose."

"Raul, that's enough."

"It makes the skin on his stump bleed."

"He has to get used to it."

Outside, cats screeched in near-human voices. A drunken man's song staggered with him down the alley, and I caught a glimpse of stars, glinting like talons, in the black sky.

"It calms him down, wearing it like that," I said. "Like he's doing what we want him to, even though he has no idea why."

"What do you know of his ideas?"

"It is what it is, Mama," I said. "Let him be. Is that so hard, to just let him be?"

The apartment grows cold, and the phone echoes silence. In the dark I see a dark creature, high shoulders sloping steeply to black haunches and a long, black tail, pacing the length of the apartment. His claws mark time, like seconds on a clock, as he travels back and forth, back and forth, across the floor. He waits for me, impatiently. Did you see him, Papa?

In the plaza, we sat on a bench, our backs to the sun. You would be dead in two weeks, the infection deep inside your bones coming back to life. I coaxed you out of your long-sleeved shirt, the one you always wore to hide the stump. I had an orange, and peeled it for the two of us, stacking the bits of rind between us. A few of the pieces of peel I held in front of our faces, noses almost touching, bent them in half so we could see the tiny gushes of orange oil.

"Can you smell it, Papa? Here, have a piece."

I pressed my thumbs into the center of the orange, pulled apart the sections with the sound of papers sliding, orange juice running down my fingers and hands. I separated one translucent crescent, lifted it up to show you. You opened your mouth, and I put it on your tongue.

"Don't forget the seed spitting contest, Papa."

You looked at me, your gaze still a foreign language. The arm was draped around your shoulders like the arm of a friend, claw resting in the center of your pale chest. Your lower legs were hidden, tucked underneath you as you sat on the bench. I shoved an orange section in my mouth, worked my tongue around a few seeds, keeping them separate while I swallowed the fruit. Then, with a giant spitting sound, better than the best old Madrileno hawking onto the street, I sent pea-sized pits five meters at least, and looked to you.

"Your turn."

You pursed your lips, an entirely different style, blew out like a machine gun, rat-a-tat-tat, each seed delivered with its own punch. I ran from the bench to see who had won. When I turned back to you, the sun was so bright behind your head I could not see your face, but I heard you, laughing.

The First Wife

Ruth Lilian

I write this from the perspective of a man of 130 years. These events happened to a youth, aged 20 years. And a youth who had no childhood, who was the one and only youth.

At that time, my garden, I made up that word for it, was like a harmony; nature was all-of-a-piece. The air was fresh, the wet grass fragrant, wild roses twined in perfect symmetry. It sounds like I'm showing off, when I get fancy with words, but it was my job to name everything. I called it language.

One very important day a creature appeared.

It was in the morning. Rain announced itself with a clack of thunder. Rain was like a foggy white mist that floated straight down, pooling on the ground. The sky was split over and over. The clouds looked dark and heavy, like rocks. A cloud dropped and the sun was gone. Wind beat the fruit trees and rain rolled over the garden in shining waves. A clump of wild bamboo waved like a centipede being tickled, one leg behind another leg behind another leg. Wolves howled.

Thunder rumbled along, rain stopped, and the air cleared.

I saw the creature under a tree, taking shelter from the rain. Long hair, like a dark vapor, spread around the creature's ankles. Curly hair, like my lamb's was, only black, with red highlights, like fire eating.

I approached and the creature was almost as tall as I, with skin the color of wet sand, smooth and smoky; a hairless face with features like my own and standing on two feet, like me, only without a trinket between the legs, but showing the beginning of a crevice decorated by black ringlets. A female me!

I was afraid the female would run away, so I took hold of the long hair. I was scared the female wouldn't like me. Never, never had I seen anything like this female, with teats that were huge, not like my little lamb's were. I didn't know what to say, although I'm a pretty good wordsmith, naming the flowers and animals and sometimes I came up with what I thought was pretty good, like Llama, and Giselle.

So in a burst, I thought up 'she' and 'her' and 'lady' and 'madam.' I said, "Madam, I'm Adam." Not to brag, even in such a time of excitement, I created the first palindrome.

She gave me a very level look with her eyes, her sparkling eyes, and my knees went atremble (I made up the word 'knees' on the spot). Only I stopped thinking of words then and there. I moved my hands around, spread them wide and waved them back and forth. "This is a garden," I said. "My garden, and now I share it with you."

I let go of her hair.

She spoke my name. "Adam."

From her obsidian eyes down to the lapis lazuli in her navel, down to her misty toes, she was beautiful. She would be mine. We would be one flesh. I thought I should go behind and mount her to become one with her. But as I turned she turned. For a while we circled round and round until I felt such desire that I didn't turn any longer but with my trinket standing straight out I entered her as we stood, face to face. Inside, she was larger than my lamb. I thrust and she thrust back, she was juicy, which I had never experienced before. I placed my hands on her belly and her skin was smoother than my lamb's. She didn't try to move away, I had no need to hold on to her. She clutched my shoulders and drew my face down and I felt her lips on mine, which had never been done before.

"Adam" she breathed, and the closeness of her... she smelled like hot pepper and bitter orange and rose geranium... not like my lamb, who used to run away from me and I had to catch her first.

Before, I was neither cheerful nor cheerless. I never questioned my duty and I always did it; named all kinds of wild things, all kinds of cattle, creeping things, every seed-bearing plant, and multiples of birds and fish. Multiples! And not much else to do, everything flourished on its own. Now, I was busy being beloved, and I no longer envied my animals; the males no longer clawed the earth when I approached and the females no longer ran away, as before I never had a suitable partner.

We had all the time in the world; she milked the goats and pounded the grains and we swam in the teeming stream with the golden fish and the four rivers rose to water the garden and I was never so productive as now.

I named Hyacinth and Behemoth and Gihon and Cush.

The funny thing was, with her, I was at a loss for words. This was not my one and only problem. Problem two, she didn't want to be fruitful and multiply; and three, she liked to lie on top. The recumbent position was denigrating to her, she said.

"Why should I always lie underneath," she complained.

"I have dominion over all the creatures," I said.

But she wouldn't listen. "You were pretty green when I met you," she said.

She would never stick to the subject.

It got annoying. I developed the first ever headache. My work suffered. I would say "heel" and she would say "head."

I tried to explain. "Words have to describe. Like Moon." I pursed my lips. "Moooon. Oooo. See? Round like the sound."

"Sometimes Moon is like a curved knife blade," she said.

"You don't understand." I said.

"Don't waggle your finger at me!"

"There's no need for you to understand. There's simply no need. Now let's talk about something else. Like, about your vegetable garden."

"How so? Talk about what?"

"I still have to name the vegetables, I'm not denying that. But that's not because you're stupid. I'm not denying you're smart. That's… no. That's wrong. I'm telling you, I'll explain where you went wrong."

Her neck went red. "You blot me out!" she screamed. And the argument continued.

I think we argued about that because we didn't argue about what really mattered. Like, why were we in the garden? What was the meaning of it?

One day I named her "Strumpet."

"Don't you bad-mouth me," she said.

"Succubus," I named her.

"You pig!" she cried.

"I'm the decider," I said. How tongue-tied she made me!

Every strand of her hair flashed fire. That night she refused me.

When I finally fell asleep, in my dream she appeared. She dangled her body in front of me. She wore bdellium in her hair; her hair twinkling like moonstone, her mouth poised as a delicate opening, tongue pointed like a sword, her thighs quivered and from her crevice nectar flowed. She grabbed and kissed me, rubbed oil over my body and poured wine, and when I awoke the ground beneath me was wet. Nocturnal emission, I named it.

I began to think of her as evil. Yet with her… she was… my home. I said the first cliché, "Home is where the heart is." I warmed myself with her, we plucked from the trees, dug up from the earth, bound flowers in each other's hair, squatted side by side by the river, took day trips to Cush, even the shrillness of her voice when we quarreled (I called her screech-owl)... I could not think of her as evil.

One night, we were lying on the green grass. Arguing only a little. My hand was tracing her nipples; plump beads. I had seen my baby animals suck from the breast and I bent over because I never had a mother and I wanted to know how this felt. She laughed and gently stroked my hair so I thought to go on with the event and flung an arm over her body and my lust grew. She plied me with her tongue... draining my life away... her tongue threaded with honey.... she fondled my trinket and that finished me... she got scratched on her buttocks from my nails and later I watched her wound heal and named the scab... I could not think of her as evil.

During a period of comparative peace, "I name you Lily," I said.

"Lilith," she said.

"Lily."

"Lilith."

And Lilith she became. This weakness of mine led to tragedy.

I was busy trimming my beard when she said, "Aren't you bored?"

"Bored is a hard word. I take my responsibility seriously."

"I'd like to leave the garden for a while."

"Leave the garden? Why?"

"Everything gets along fine without us."

"We're the caretakers of the garden."

"I want to travel."

"I have obligations, I have things yet to name, all the time new things come up."

"Sir Namer, for once in your life, be carefree."

"I have to keep dominion over the animals."

"That's no reason, Sir Dominion, to keep us here."

This was a new habit of hers. Sir Dominion, Sir Namer, Sir We-have-to. The words rolled in her mouth like sweet-meats.

"What do we need all this for?" she said scornfully.

"Because we have to." This came out of my mouth before I could suppress it.

"Every time I start to talk to you, you throw in a 'have to.' Like what do we have to?"

"There's a bare spot in the garden, and we have to dead-head the flowers, and I'm making a new kind of broom, and..."

"For all eternity, I've got to listen to a babbler."

"And," I played my trump card. "We have to stop living irresponsibly and have to have children."

"I'm going anyway."

"I'm the man, I have the beard, and I have the final word," I said.

She spoke strangely and unexpectedly. "I refuse to accept your phallicism." This was no word of mine and my spirit grew dark with fury.

Again I attempted celibacy but Lilith was always in my night sheet with the tang of myrrh and cassia.

I took to spying on her. She liked to move about in the darkness. She would play with the owls and jackals and kites, leaning over them like a crescent moon, cross-legged, her face hidden by her hair. She allowed the serpent to caress her with his long body; he wove himself around her thighs and slid up her breast and hissed at the nipples. And perhaps he drank from her breast, which I had not accomplished.

"Lascivious demon!" I cried. By this time I had many names for her.

Next morning she wore smaragdos in her navel and in her hair she wore a tiny snake like a crown.

I found no words to confront her. My head was burning with ice hotter than fire.

That night I tried to force her and she screamed a word I had never heard. In a rage, (she had a terrible temper), she said, "I will fly to the Red Sea to live in a cave!" and she ran off.

It was on the fifth moon of the second year that Lilith deserted me and the garden. My aloneness was painful, like a chunk of my happiness was obliterated. All was quiet except for an occasional bleat or tweet; all was serene, perfect, sunny and blooming. For a while I just hung around. I even eyed my lamb as she nibbled on the green grass, but it wouldn't have been the same. I neglected myself, my beard needed trimming and I stank. Why bother?

I named Jelly fish and Cockroach. Why bother?

I became lethargic. I made up "spite" as in "cut off your nose to spite your face." I became mean. I squashed a lady bug, looked to the Heavens expecting a clap, or, at least a cloud, but the bright sun didn't even blink.

Demons visited me at night. Nocturnal emissions rained over the garden. It was terrifying. I stopped sleeping.

I thought to go to the Red Sea and bring Lilith back.

So I walked out of the garden, over the hills, past the tamarisks in the sandy tracts, into the desert. I heard distant lowing of the gazelles and the wild cows, heard the camel's harsh cries as they mated, the jackals howling. And I was alone. I remembered Lilith's long nails scraping my back

I continued walking. I ate nettles and unnamed plants and was ashamed, so I quickly said, "Cactus and sagebrush." I remembered how we ate eggplant and almond-sprinkled custard.

Slowly, the landscape changed to giant sandstone rocks carved by wind-driven grit into grotesque shapes. I remembered when the wind was music.

I was not self-analytical but I was feeling tremendous fear that I must never do this horrible thing; I must not leave the ordained way of life.

However, my heels didn't heed my head. As I dully plodded on, I began to speculate on what I would find at the Red Sea.

The water of the Red Sea was pure and I splashed and felt it seeping down the length of my aching legs. I put my head down and drank, my eyes open to see the beautiful blue around me.

When I raised my dripping head I saw what surely were demons. One was a female, laughing, wet and glistening; all I could see of her was the start of a rounded and generous ass, and her flowing hair that floated on the surface of the Red Sea.

An enormous spear (my new name for his, which surpassed any trinket I had ever seen) was attached to a muscular demonic male, making his way slowly towards her. His legs were in the water, but his torso was evident. His torso was all interlocked wedges, two chest muscles above a wedge of a stomach above the aforementioned spear hanging between two bristled sacs. He was not the golden brown I was, but was bright red as a ripe apple.

I couldn't compare the rest of him to myself; I had no true idea what I looked like.

He approached, spear in the forefront, red and bouncing with each step, like the forceful branch of a mighty tree, ending in a taut bulb.

The female demon turned to one side. I saw her profile. Lilith! The male demon reached her, placed one arm around her tapered waist, and his arm slid down the softness of her ass to disappear in the Sea. A wide grin on his face, there was a plunge downward of his enormous chest, and slowly, his eyes closed and he thrust his head under the water.

The water around her belly churned, Lilith swirled, and ecstatically moaned. She threw back her head, thrust her ass backwards, her eyes rolled upward, and she licked her moistened lips. She seemed to sink into the water and all I could see was the tendrils of her hair as she was whipped about, to and fro. He surfaced, leering with pleasure, and then re-submerged. She bobbed like a cork.

What emotions I had I will not attempt to describe.

I fought against the knowledge of what was going on, but, in profile, I could see Lilith's nipple was bulging so I knew she was enjoying whatever it was. Thus passed a few minutes; both of them emerging, submerging, emerging, submerging, until, in an explosion of water, he was elevated high in the air and I could see his swollen spear, full unto bursting, and then I, myself, let go with a violent shout, and that stopped him short.

In such a moment, when I would have expected my intellect to be silent, my mind coined "*coitus interruptus.*"

Now, Lilith was above water and both were standing; he crouched in fighting attitude and she with her hand to her mouth. "Adam!" she shrieked.

They sloshed to shore, he with his spear all dangling and wrinkled.

When I reached them I realized I had been under misapprehension brought about by my own imagination; he was merely a taller male with a hairy chest of matted red hair. He postured a bit, flexed some muscles, but he didn't seem to have the gift of language and spoke only with his eyes. It was Lilith who sang out:

"Very nice, Sir Namer, very nice. You made it, you left the garden."

Have I told you about her voice? I never found a word for it, it was quivering and hollow, like air blown through a reed, yet it was wide and full, and also mellow and deep. That's why I never found a word for it.

She sat down on the sandy shore, stared at me, at him, at me. Her voice trembled. "Then I really have a problem."

Under the sun, Lilith's body was a dotted landscape of shimmering beads of water flowing over hills and leas, gathering at the narrow ravine between her swelling breasts, becoming threads rushing to join and enter her pink crevice, as mysterious as a grotto.

Dazzled as I was, a hard fact came to me. Above the enticing crevice and under the blue-veined breasts, the soft belly was more than rounded, it was curving outward.

Lilith was fruitful!

Whose seed had been planted? Mine or his? How could I know? Even if I remembered how long she'd been absent from me, I didn't know the period of gestation for a human. Ah, but was this the first human pregnancy or was it cross-breeding?

Meanwhile Lilith placed her hands under the stomach containing my, his, seed. And I ground my teeth, should I be furious or happy?

Smack in the gut the answer came. Ask her, she should know.

"Lilith!" I exploded. "Is this to be Adam junior, or what?"

"I'm going to have many babies," she yelled back, "and all of them will be little Liliths."

"You... sorceress!" I shouted. I knew she was provoking me, she always liked a good fight. "What's the matter with you? Wasn't I good to you? Why was it always I want I want I want to be on top I want to make up language I want to design the Garden I want to I want to I want to."

"I wanted what was mine by right."

"What was wrong?" I was almost crying with happiness, the old habit came back so naturally, both of us at full throttle, me laying down the rules and she objecting. Momentarily I glanced at the demon, shuffling aimlessly, looking less and less potent.

Coitus interruptus, I told myself, doesn't lead to fruitfulness.

Soon Lilith and I would be back at the Garden, and she'd give birth. I wouldn't punish her for being unfaithful. I had also been unfaithful with the lamb.

Lilith stopped speaking in the middle of a word beginning with the sound *jsh.*

She wrung droplets from her hair, and they trickled into the stream leading to her grotto. "Adam, it's different here. They've invented play. They invented cuisine. They dress. They invented leisure."

"While you were gone, *I* invented law."

"They invented birth control," she snapped. "I didn't use it. I was having too good a time." She raised her eyebrows. Rubbed her belly as if it contained a delicious meal.

Tired as I was, I reacted immediately. My brain seemed to throb, then with an open hand I smote her face.

Lilith hooted. "Sir Bully!"

Strangely, the demon did nothing.

I waited.

Lilith said to me, "He could squash you like a grape."

I threw myself at the demon with a mightily clenched fist and I knocked out his front tooth. He neither defended himself nor attacked back. His tongue explored his bleeding mouth; he rubbed his finger over his lips and stared at his blood, sorrowfully.

He shook his head back and forth, a silent no no no no no.

I was still trembling, still waiting for him to lunge at me, when Lilith put her hand over his heart and using all the aspects of her voice said to him, "Don't worry. I could never go back after all that has happened here."

With a roar of, "You're mine!" I spurted to his side. Then did the demon tower over me, still spitting blood, showing his gaping maw of gum. I set my own teeth together and swung my fist at his chin; he seized my wrist. I tried to free my arm, he hung on, I tugged, he pulled, I raised my arm, he lowered it, I tried with my other arm, he seized that wrist, I dropped to my knees, he dropped to his knees, I tried twisting; we swayed sideways, rocked back and forth, rolled over and over, in and out of the Red Sea. Pebbles and sand stuck to our sweaty bodies, by now we were both coughing salt water and gasping air.

I realized Lilith, for some time, had been laughing at us.

He realized it at the same time and let go my wrists. We both sat, panting heavily.

Beside us the Red Sea shimmered and glittered. It was truly a lovely spot. A sand crab sidled by and dug itself a hole near my big toe. I sat, my tongue hanging out, panting and snarling like a dog. Lilith joined us, sat in the middle, unafraid. As my breath returned, my mind returned and I experienced the first self-doubt of my short life.

I had appeared ridiculous.

She was whispering in his ear. He shook his head, she whispered, he showed his bloody teeth in a smile.

It's rude to whisper. I was itching to teach them I was not to be disrespected. However, looking at his swelling mouth and her darkening eye, both of my doing, I had no heart to speak.

United by his arm about her shoulders and hers around his waist, they got to their feet as if one person. All my lust turned to hatred. I was filled with hatred. I spurned her, I spurned him, I turned my back on both of them and strode off on the tortuous return to the Garden.

She shouted to me, "Goodbye and good luck, Sir Inventor. I won't forget you." Her last words evaporated into the Red Sea.

In essence, what I found at the Red Sea was an unanswered question.

How could I have dominion over my animals if I behaved like an animal?

I got home. Nothing had changed except for more weeds in the Garden. I plucked them out. For a while I was not myself and coupled like a madman. Gazelles, cows, goats, sheep-- once I even lay in the mud with the pigs-- and suffered erectile dysfunction. I was deeply unhappy in that unstructured and mindless period of my life although I could still turn a pretty phrase and the constant running after animals kept me in excellent shape.

Soon any animal catching my scent immediately bolted and I was left to my nocturnal emissions. I decided it was not good for me to cast my seed upon the ground. No doubt I was maturing. That was good. I found I liked declaring what was good or not good. I took to the task gratefully to fill up the endless time. I made up meal times and bed times and I made up obedience. And I said a sorceress is not good. And any one who lies with an animal is not good. And all those animals that lack fins or scales are not good. A grasshopper is good and an owl is not good. The rat and the gecko are not good. And the female blood that came from the crevice is not good and the female cannot be approached until seven days have passed. And the flow from the trinket is good (unless it spills on the ground). To trim the edge of the beard is not good. The adulteress is not good, she has no one to blame but herself. Cleanliness is good and fine flour is good. And frankincense is good. The rat and the gecko are not good and snakes are not good. The pig is definitely not good. Lambs are good. Six days of work is good. Seven is not good.

I kept on and on deciding what was good; and it was good. I called it religion.

Soon self-doubt came again. Was I right in naming what was good or not good? I worried what would happen to all my unused seed, piling up inside of me.

For advice there was none to consult. The animals were simple-minded except for the snake who quickly stuck out his tongue at me when I asked him to consider my problems.

I was afraid to sleep, thinking Lilith would visit me. At night I slept with my hands over my trinket to prevent it from rising.

One night it rained most heavily, mosquitoes came, not good, and the ground turned to clay. It was a restless night for me, with disturbing dreams of danger from unknown sources. Finally morning came. I woke up suddenly to see the growing light define another she walking towards me, with mud on her feet.

Her lips were red as sour cherries. I rose and she reached only as high as my ribs. I extended my hand to her and she knelt before me. I found an empty space in my heart for her.

My second wife, Eve, the acquiescent one, who exercised her power over me by manipulation, not confrontation, I didn't care, it was better than confrontation, she made me eat of the apple, and after that you know what happened.

SEA OF TRANQUILLITY

Beverly Akerman

There's a quality to this silence that makes me think I should have faked it tonight.

"You okay, Hannah?" Cal says into the darkness.

"Yeah, don't worry about it," I say. "Must be the phase of the moon or something."

We face one another, feet touching in the middle of the bed, our bodies forming a misshapen heart. Each of us has the white sheet tucked under an arm.

"Hannah? You sure?"

"Yes," I answer, a shade too emphatic.

He reaches out and grazes my cheek with a finger.

I pull my head back, say goodnight, turn away. He moves closer, tucking under me until we're spooning. It isn't long until I hear his breathing deepen and elongate, cresting like ocean waves.

I close my eyes, try to sleep, knowing very well I cannot. The clock reads two-fifty-seven a.m. I reach for the small pill I left on the night table, just in case. It glows red in the light from the digital display; I've only recently figured out how to take it without water.

A neighbour's cat yowls. I picture the moon, lowering over the horizon. Cal turns over, rustling the sheets. Tomorrow. Maybe tomorrow I'll tell him I'm leaving, if I can think of someplace to go. I've tried not to make a big deal of it, thought it was temporary, an erotic hiccup. But it's been a couple of months now since I've been able to come. I've taken it as some kind of sign, promised myself I would leave, finally, if things didn't improve. There have to be consequences; what's missing is too basic, like the steel girders that hold a skyscraper upright. I can't just go on pretending nothing has changed.

At first, I did fake an orgasm or two, but eventually Cal noticed. And that hangdog look he'd given me, well, *that* had been too much, beyond the limit. Surprising, really, given everything else I've managed to live through. It isn't anything Cal has done, or left undone, more like some primitive lizard-brain circuit has broken. It's not something I'm aware of having chosen.

Cal's a software engineer. On a good day, he calls himself a code jock. We actually work at the same university though in different departments, a coincidence we discovered that first night at the Lamplighters. He's short and chunky, with a dimple on his right cheek and dirty blond hair. I usually find nail-biting a disgusting habit, but somehow with Cal I don't mind it so much.

Waiting for the pill to kick in, I crave distraction--insomnia's as much fun as sticking pins in my eyes--but it's the middle of the night. Outside it's silent as the grave. Then I remember the news today, that glimpse of my last childhood icon, the giant Guaranteed Pure Milk bottle. The Mayor's decided it's got to go, after years spent rusting away, untended, the company defunct, in an area of downtown aching for renewal. I've always loved it, this piece of genuine Montreal kitsch, propped up on scaffolding ten stories high, tilted to the side as though just about to pour.

Every Tuesday and Thursday afternoon when I was growing up, the Guaranteed Pure Milk Company would deposit two bottles, two percent butterfat, at the door of the upper duplex where we lived. And in the winter, when I returned from school at the end of the day, a glacial column of milk would have pushed the white, green, and orange cardboard tops up and out from the glass bottles. My mother never seemed to remember to come down and get them.

In those days, my family took in foster kids, my mother's idea, like most that went on in my family. She'd read some heart-melting newspaper article about unwanted kids, and then talked and talked and talked till dad finally said okay. He'd kick up a fuss sometimes but ultimately agreed to just about anything she asked of him. The social worker showed up the very next day. Maybe Mom didn't know no good deed goes unpunished.

Though we weren't well off, my parents didn't do it for the money. In fact, I'm pretty sure we lost on the deal. They were always giving those kids more than the agency saw fit to provide. Like the time thirteen-year-old Colin wanted sealskin boots, "like everybody else had." Sealskin boots were the kind of thing you just had to have, to fit in back in 1968. Not that they indulged me that way, gave me the things I thought I *had* to have. Like those white go-go boots that ended just below the calf, zippers up the back finishing in large gold hoops. The agency paid for a foster kid's boots, sure, but not for *sealskin* boots, so my parents made up the difference. Maybe it was because they felt bad for the kid, having lost his family and all. Maybe they thought if they couldn't give him his family back, the least they could do was make sure he got those boots. I hadn't really minded though, Colin getting his dream boots when I didn't get mine. Even then I recognized it was a fair enough trade.

Two years now I've been with Cal, since a little after Molly died. I met him at a Lamplighters meeting, 'support and self-help for bereaved parents.' His marriage hadn't survived his son's passing, either. Four-years-old. Leukemia. Before it happened, I would have predicted nothing could be more depressing than sitting in a room filled with grieving parents and grandparents, sometimes brothers and sisters, too. But I would have been wrong.

Life had been perfect then, but I'd just been too busy to notice, the universally fatal lapse. My daughter Molly was something special, not quite three, with a perfect rosebud mouth, a messy crown of chestnut curls and a laugh that helped me finally get the point of those feng shui waterfalls. Such a little thing, I never would've believed she could open that door off the kitchen.

She'd always been an early riser; it was a source of friction between Eric and me. We'd tried 'Ferberizing' her, lying in the basement holding each other as she screamed her lungs out. But I couldn't do it, didn't have the necessary ruthlessness to be that kind of parent. We consulted the pediatrician about Molly's sleep patterns several times, desperate for some strategy that would allow us, finally, to sleep past five-thirty in the blessed a.m. "Don't worry, she'll come round eventually," we'd be told as we sat there, bleary-eyed, while little Molly chirruped and gambolled.

That morning—I'll never forget it-- I woke with a start. Glanced at the clock: eight-twenty-five a.m. We hadn't slept in like that for months, years maybe. For a moment I luxuriated in it, stretching like a cat. I felt so good, like I might finally be in control of my own life again. Car doors slammed, kids called out to one another on their way to school, a lawn mower started up in the distance. Sunlight sifted round the edges of the curtains, filling the room with a lemony glow. A cardinal was singing. Maybe Molly was settling down to a reasonable schedule, I thought. Finally. Had to happen sometime, didn't it? I rolled over and kissed Eric, snuggled a hand down, caressed him awake. He said what he always said when our daughter did something exceptional: "good golly, Miss Molly." We stayed there together another half-hour or so, enjoying a little mental health day celebration.

I was the one who found her, floating, face down, just after nine. We'd had an above ground pool installed earlier that spring. It was the only time she ever managed to get out of the crib on her own.

Cal turns over, tossing a leaden arm over me. I push it off, but gently. Shifting onto my back, I sigh. I try the deep, diaphragmatic breathing my therapist taught me, counting down, ten in, hold it one-two-three, ten out. I finish all ten breaths, but still there's a knot in my gut. I pinch the bridge of my nose with thumb and forefinger, screw my eyes tight, but I do not cry. Something else, there has to be something else.

When I was a kid, I walked to school and back, lunchtimes too. I'd meander, especially in winter, taking my time, kicking through the slush at the edge of the street, clearing a careful path for the snowmelt to reach the sewers. It left me feeling virtuous, even civic-minded. One Tuesday, I arrived home after one of my massive water diversion projects to find the milk bottles missing. I opened the door with my key and slowly climbed the long, dark staircase. At the top, as usual, I kicked off my boots – my shoes remained stuck in their detested bottoms – and was gratified to hear them clunk their way down, hitting every step, coming to rest against the front door where my dad, as the next scheduled arrival, would have to push them aside. But he never minded things like that, the things kids did that annoyed most grown-ups; he was good that way.

My socks shimmied half-off, I imagined myself as Godzilla stumping down the hallway toward the kitchen, sing-songing "hi Mom, I'm ho-ome," as though anyone could possibly have missed the commotion. Mom was in the kitchen, as usual, but there was this little kid perched on the Formica countertop, hunched over as though trying to disappear, as though trying to make herself as inconspicuous as possible. It offended me; we weren't allowed to sit up there. There was something about this kid, though, something that kept me from saying anything. The milk bottles glistened beside her, covered in rivulets of condensation.

"The social worker brought them in," my mom said as she caught me staring at them. She put a hand on the girl's head. "This is Cindy. She's going to stay with us awhile."

"Hey Cin," I said, shrugging out of my jacket and snow pants. The kid bowed her head, then looked up at me, her eyebrows knitted together.

"Where'll she sleep?" I asked. My mother looked at me. There were just the three bedrooms. My parents had one; my sister's was more like a closet. And then there was mine.

-

"In a sleeping bag on the floor for tonight. We'll get bunk beds tomorrow, hopefully."

The agency must have promised them. "Can I sleep on top?"

"We'll see, honey."

I couldn't take my eyes off this kid, there was something funny about her. Her mouth, it looked smudged somehow; the two halves didn't meet cleanly in the middle. One side looked as thought it had been folded on top of the other and pressed in place.

"What's with her mouth?"

"She has cleft lip and palate. That means her lip and the roof of her mouth didn't form properly when she was growing in her Mummy's tummy. But they've already operated on her once and when she gets older, they'll fix it so you'd never know."

"How old are you anyway, Cindy?"

A moment's silence. My mom smoothed the girl's messy hair: "she's five, but she looks a bit younger, don't you sweetie? They said it was an emergency, that they couldn't leave her at home for one second longer."

I looked Cindy over again--white baby shoes, horizontally patterned jersey snapped at the neck. She *was* awfully small, dressed more like a toddler than a kid who belonged in kindergarten. A diaper lurked beneath the grey corduroys, her hair looked like it hadn't been washed in a while. And she still hadn't uttered a word.

"Can't she talk?"

"Of *course* she can talk. She's just shy, that's all. Aren't you Cindy?" My mom gave her a squeeze but Cindy stiffened, snuffled loudly, and erupted in a phlegmy cough. Yuck, I thought, somebody better get this kid with the program.

"C'mon Cindy," I said, picking her up and snuggling her onto my hip. I had younger cousins, was already an old hand at babysitting. "She can have my bed Mom, okay? I'll sleep on the floor."

"Wanna walk," Cindy said, so I put her down. I felt a wisp of a hand slip into my own.

"I'll show you your new room, you're sharing with me. Did you know there's a full moon tonight? We'll go out later on and I'll show you, okay?"

Cindy wouldn't look at me but she nodded, putting her fingers in her mouth like she wanted to jam the whole hand in there.

A few weeks before Molly died, we'd decided we were ready for another baby. After the drowning, Eric fixated on a new baby like a starving man on an all-you-can-eat buffet. But as time went on, I realized I couldn't do it, couldn't have that baby. Just knew it, the way you know about gravity before anyone's ever explained it. And I knew nothing Eric could say would change my mind; he'd begun to seem more and more like a mirage to me anyway at that point, our marriage too--hazy, indistinct, maybe not even really there. When I finally told him how I felt, that I'd secretly gone back on the Pill, the light leaked out of his eyes completely. That night he packed and left--I wasn't sorry, exactly. Anyway, I'd studied physics. It was inevitable, like a Newtonian principle: for every action, an equal and opposite reaction.

Soon as I could, I went back to work. Medical research. As a student, it seemed so altruistic but in practice, it came down to decapitating mice and fishing out their intestines for molecular transport experiments. It took a lot of concentration and a lot of equipment: cages, balances, water baths, shakers, flasks, medium, test-tubes and pipettes, alcohol, dry ice, a round fluorescent magnifying loop with a hinged arm, a miniature guillotine of stainless steel, scalpels, and a host of other sharp instruments. I was relieved to lose myself in something so absorbing, grateful not to have too many of my own neurons floating around, underused. And three nights a week, I went to Lamplighter meetings in musty church basements all over Montreal. They never force anyone to tell their story, or even to talk at all. A person could just sit there all night, only listening, drinking a scalding liquid that tasted more like melted brown crayons than coffee, so that's what I did. I never cried. I just tried to make sure I never went home alone to that empty house. The pool had been done away with even before Molly's funeral; somebody's brother-in-law took it down, I think. I was pretty doped up; the details are mercifully obscure.

Cal's the only one who's made me feel much of anything, since it happened. I have no idea why; he doesn't seem much different from any of the others I brought home. But every once in a while when I'm with him, even if for the briefest instant, I get the feeling that maybe my life hasn't already ended, that maybe some kind of future is still possible.

Cindy bloomed in our family circle, her baby shoes soon traded up for classic, red-leather Mary Janes. One spring morning, we both woke early. When I checked, Cindy's diaper was dry, so we rigged up the toilet seat insert and she gave it a go. The smile on that kid's face as she heard her own tinkles, so broad it looked like her upper lip might tear apart again. I found a pair of honeycomb-quilted training pants in a bureau drawer and told her she was a big girl. "You can wear underwear, just like everybody else. No more diapers."

I was as proud as she was.

Then one night, my mom went to the movies with a friend, leaving dad to take care of us girls. At bedtime, he scooped Cindy up, the littlest one, tucking her under one arm. "Let's read *Good night moon,*" he said, "okay, young lady?"

"No," Cindy answered in a tiny voice, struggling a little in his arms. "Let me go," she whispered. Either he didn't hear her or he didn't get it, I was never sure which. Maybe he thought she just didn't want to go to bed; I've always had the feeling dads could be kind of dense.

"Let me *go,*" Cindy repeated.

Dad kept on walking toward the bedroom, whistling, oblivious, till Cindy threw up. At first, we thought it was a virus or something, but it kept happening, whenever my dad tried to do something with her. Then came the day when dad put Cindy on his lap to tie her shoelaces and she wet her pants. And this was after six months without any diapers. Mom called the social worker. Something had happened between Cindy and her father, though I was never told what, exactly. I just got a long lecture from my mom, about not talking to strangers, especially strange men, about never leaving Cindy alone outside.

Another day, I rounded the corner after school in time to see a police car peeling from the curb in front of our house. It was the first time I ever felt my heart fall, transformed into a sick knot of grief. For a moment, I stood there, then ran the rest of the way home, throat tight, my head pounding, and rushed inside to find Cindy in my mom's lap, in the rocking chair, mom wiping her own tears away and Cindy howling, inconsolable. The police had taken Cindy's father. He'd shown up to bellow and rage at the front door, his fury echoing, amplifying their terror, as it mounted the long, dark staircase.

After that, I spent even more time with the kid, talking, reading stories, teaching her to play jacks and other simple games with cards or a ball, things any normal five-year-old girl could do. It was 1969, and the infinite universe was my new passion, the sky, the planets and the stars. For the science fair, Cindy helped me make a model solar system, covering foam balls with papier mâchée, painting them, rigging little motors that spun them round their axes. My project made the finals in the regional competition and this so impressed my parents, they gave me a small telescope to mark the occasion. We gazed at the stars and the moon, tried to locate the Sea of Tranquillity. I taught Cindy to recognize the Big Dipper, that the sun was a giant ball of fire.

Cal's dreaming. "No, *no,*" he says. Then something I can't catch, something not quite words. He's too close now, making me feel too warm. I try to put more distance between us. As if that's possible. Cal's a good man. Has a stutter his parents spent thousands trying to cure him of. He told me it only showed up when he was tired or stressed, which, when I think about it, should have been all the time, at least since I've known him. But maybe not. Maybe after the worst happens, the thing you can't even imagine, you relax, sort of. Maybe there's a version of freedom that comes with being pre-disastered.

We don't talk much. I've heard him describe those twin deaths, his son and his marriage. I've felt him inside me. What more do I need to know? It's enough that he's gentle, that he's here. Not much of a life, Cal and me, but for a while there, it seemed like enough, an acceptable form of limbo. Or is that purgatory? My theology's a little rusty.

How naïve the young are, how complacent, believing they deserve success, their good fortune, because they're good people, doing everything right. That when bad things happen, it's just karma, because 'what goes around comes around.' Positively Old Testament, isn't it, an eye for an eye and all that. Amazing, really, anyone can still see at all. Nothing more than a shared delusion, the idea there's any justice in this universe. There isn't. I know. I've looked for it. Everywhere.

The waif with dirty hair and baby clothes grew six inches and gained eleven pounds in the short time she'd been with us; the social worker was pleased. Cindy was doing well in kindergarten, reading even. And we'd become inseparable. I was closer to that kid than I'd ever been to my 'real' sister, closer than I would be to anyone else, ever. And that, I know, was the original sin.

Early summer, Sunday, five p.m. The two of us begged to go to the park before dinner. It was a languid afternoon; the house smelled like roast beef and apple pie. My mom didn't want us to go but our chores were done, I pointed out, and my homework. I was pretty relentless and she finally gave in, telling me to take my watch, to be home for six-thirty.

At the park, we threw ourselves into it, climbing the jungle gym (though I was afraid of heights), making mud pies in the sandbox, tumbling down a grassy slope over and over again, laughing. Everything was lush, green and blooming, full of possibility. School was almost over; I was teaching Cindy the chant 'no more pencils, no more books, no more teacher's dirty looks.' She giggled every time she said it; she loved being naughty. I could have sworn there was perfection in the slant of the light as the day began to fade. We were on the swings. A persimmon smear filled the sky.

"Six-thirty kid, time to go," I said.

"Can't we touch the moon Hannah, just once more? Pretty please?"

Sometimes a sliver of moon appeared in the sky, and we'd imagine that if we went high enough, we'd sail into space, be the first girls in history to set foot on the moon. It was our irresistible, secret fantasy, and so I gave in, in love with my role as indulgent older sister even though I knew we should be leaving. Then Cindy asked if, instead of swinging side-by-side, we could swing together, so I put her on my lap, holding her close. Cindy in my right hand, the swing in my left, I flew through space, hair streaming, legs pumping.

"Higher," Cindy shouted, "higher."

And there we were, stretching our legs out, doing our damnedest to touch the moon. Cindy squealed and suddenly we were pivoting, slipping backward, tumbling down to earth. I fought to stay upright, to keep hold of the swing, to make sure that if anyone hit the dirt it would be me alone, that Cindy would only thump harmlessly against me. And in that, at least, I was successful.

I lay flat on my back, dust rising, gob smacked. The swing jangled against the metal post, miles above me. Cindy was crying, my head hurt, my back hurt, my *everything* hurt; I may even have passed out for a moment. The swing set looked bizarre, strangely distant, like the walls did when I had a fever or lay in bed late at night, over-excited about something and unable to sleep. Winded, I struggled to catch my breath. And then from an eternity above us, from so far it away they might have come from outer space, two arms reached down to pull Cindy from my clasp. And even though I'd never seen him before I knew it was her father. And I just . . . let her go. We were two young girls, alone and vulnerable. I've told myself every day since then that there wasn't a thing I could do about it, but I will always know the truth.

Five a.m.; the sun might be rising but I do my best not to acknowledge it.

Anorgasmia--I looked it up– can be primary or secondary. More frequent in women than men, often caused by antidepressants, sexual inhibition, prostate surgery, sexual trauma. Not quite the end of the world, as I well know, having lived more than once through the end of the world.

Cal rolls toward me, reaches out and curls himself round me; we're spooning again. "Enough tossing and turning," he says, "we're on the way back up, you know we are." He murmurs this into the nape of my neck, kissing me there as though sealing a promise; it makes me shiver. And suddenly the whole thing--what he's said and the way he's said it, the kiss, the shiver, this whole long night--all resonate inside me somewhere, like tumblers turning in a lock. Then I feel it--sleep staking its claim, moving through my bloodstream, merciful, like forgiveness, flowing from wherever it's been sequestered inside me. And all at once it's so easy, falling asleep, like slipping away into the clear blue sky. And I realize that maybe I shouldn't leave Cal just yet, maybe there is something between us. That even the smallest something is worth more than a whole lot of nothing.

We did get several phone calls from the kid, crying and missing us, in the weeks after she disappeared. Cindy's father must have placed them, trying to calm her down maybe, or trying to drive us all crazy, who understands such people? They never did find her, not even a trace. Just about killed my mother. Cured her forever of foster kids.

At breakfast one morning a couple of years later, mom let out a cry as she dropped the container of milk. She stood there, a hand over her mouth. I thought she was watching the mess as it spread across the linoleum, but it was Cindy's photo she was looking at, there on the milk carton, under the caption 'missing.'

For years afterward, I'd lie outside on summer nights with my telescope and aim for tranquillity. I'd trace the Big Dipper, stare at the cold-hot stars, wondering where Cindy was. Imagining --praying? – the kid was somehow safe and loved, that maybe she was gazing up at the same sky I was. That maybe she was thinking of, remembering, someone like me.

Tea with the Editor

~

Gilda M. Haber

One sunny morning in May of 1945, two letters arrived at the White House. The White House, our gracious 500-year-old white-stone mansion in the tiny village of Great Chesterford, Essex, had become during the war, a Jewish children's refugee hostel. I was not a refugee I was British born of British-born parents, but I was Jewish.

Evacuated from London bombing for four years from 1939 to 1943, billeted with nine successive Christian country foster parents, Mummy saw I was becoming a Christian. While totally irreligious, she wished me to remain Jewish, out of London, and away from home.

Mummy was not the usual fond, doting, Jewish mother. Even though bombing had tapered off and many loving London parents had called their evacuee children home, bombing or no bombing, Mummy enjoyed her wartime evening parties. Daddy, shy and deaf, a bookworm, never joined her. She was free. But a child hampered her social life. The refugee hostel would restore my 'Jewish identity,' get me out of any London bombing, and out of her parties. My absence would relieve her of the embarrassment of my budding teen breasts.

"I didn't know you had a daughter of fourteen," friends said.

She wanted to keep it that way. Finding me a Jewish place in the country would kill two birds with one stone.

The only Jewish places outside the London bombing area were Jewish refugee homes for children. Always resourceful, Mummy found The White House refugee home. Among the thirty or so refugee children, I was the only British-born girl. However, at the White House, I gained for the first time during the war caring, protective guardians, the Shapiros, stability, good friends and a shiny Jewish identity. For the first time during the war I was happy.

The arrival of not one, but two letters that bright summer day was an added pleasure. One, a flimsy blue airmail letter came from America, the other, a thick, creamy envelope came from an unknown British writer. I did not recognize the return address. Who could have sent it?

The other children, European refugees, their relatives missing, rarely received letters. The smaller children crowded round me.

"Open them, open them," they urged.

I turned the two missives over in my hands, fingers exploring the blue airmail, soft and flexible, the creamy, pre-war envelope, thick and firm. On the blue airmail letter, I recognized the handwriting of my American pen pal, Frank Robinson, and his New York return address, but the elegant handwriting on the cream envelope mystified me.

"Who could they be from?" the small children asked, pressing their warm little bodies against mine, in the front hall. "Don't you want to see?"

Selma and Helga, my two best friends, aged respectively 15 and 14, Cookie, my thirteen-year old bête noir and I, 'the Big Girls,' all callously abandoned the smaller children's white, upturned faces. The Big Girls and I ran up the wide, curved, oak stairway, then up the next narrow smaller set of stairs to 'The Big Girls' Room' at the top of the mansion. A large, airy attic, it must once have been the maids' quarters or a nursery. Sunlight from the huge bay window flooded the room with golden light. A cozy window seat the length of the wide window, overlooked the mansion's immense green park. Hidden under dense foliage stood a small derelict greenhouse-my secret retreat- packed with ancient photos of the past, happy, White House family. Further down, a little wooden bridge spanned the pond in which stood a graceful stone sea horse. Children stood on the bridge throwing crumbs to the goldfish, the fish's orange noses darting up. At the far end of the garden, hidden from the attic's view, I imagined I could hear the deep green orchard leaves rustling, protecting their ripe apples and plums.

As we dashed into the Big Girls' room, Marta, a refugee, groomed before the war to join a Czech ballet company, stood erect against the rough bar practicing pirouettes.

I flung myself onto the window seat, and carefully opened Frank's letter, glued shut at the edges by the censors. The censor had not blacked out any of Frank's words.

As blackbirds and yellow butterflies flew past the bay window, I glanced out over the endless tranquil green with its calm pool, statuary, frolicking children, and it seemed as if there had never been six years of war and bombing. Only yesterday, brilliant fireworks shooting into the sky celebrating VE day, the defeat of Germany and victory in Europe, we had danced in the streets. The one remaining enemy was Japan. We were full of hope for peace-and for us British evacuees and soldiers-a return home to London.

"Who's it from, who's it from?' screamed Cookie, trying to snatch the blue letter from my hand. Cookie, at 13, three years my junior, a horrid prankster, had arrived in England on the *Kindertransport*. Her parents had escaped to Hong Kong. I did not know the fate of the other children's parents. Because I felt guilty being the only girl with a whole family and with two letters, I tolerated Cookie's annoying pranks.

"The blue airmail is from my American pen-pal, Frank Robinson, and the other," I turned over the creamy, thick envelope, "is a mystery; certainly not from my mother."

As the London bombing increased over six years, Mummy's writing had become

increasingly spidery. The other letter's writing was even. A stranger had written to me.

"Well, what *does* Frank say?" Marta asked. Looking like a Dègas, she executed an entrechat at the makeshift bar. All the big girls knew about Frank Robinson.

It was 1945. *Life Magazine* had published Frank's letter saying that racism against Negroes in America was undemocratic. I had written back to the magazine agreeing with Frank. The magazine forwarded my letter to him in America, and we became pen pals. I was curious about America, and liked the Yank airmen we met at their two air bases.

Selma, Helga, Cookie and I daily traveled 15 miles to the nearest high school in Bishops Stortford. En route, we met Yanks who boarded and left the train at two American air force bases: Audley End and Stanford. The boyish Yanks laughed a lot, and treated us schoolgirls, in spite of our stodgy uniforms, as young women. But once, when I told the Yanks in our carriage about Frank's letter against segregation, a thin soldier had leapt to his feet and shouted, "I'd like to stick a knife into every nigger's heart."

"That's a horrible thing to say," I'd answered, and we girls all rose to leave the carriage. This was our first encounter with what we later learned to call racism.

"So read the letters," Cookie said, as if it were her business. I'd opened Frank's.

"Dear Gilda," (I read aloud)

"This is a confession. For a long time I denied that I was Jewish. I kept it a secret but you have made me acknowledge my heritage. I admit that I am Jewish."

"Girls, girls," Cookie screamed, "Frank Robinson is Jewish!"

"I'm amazed, too," I said. "We've been writing for months, and he never said so."

"Now you can marry him," Selma said, dreamily, lying on her army cot, hands behind her head. Selma, at 15 was tall, with a full bosom, tiny waist, soft hips, shapely long legs, and shoulder-length hair, all of which I envied, though I had more admirers.

"Let me see the letter," Cookie shouted, snatching it out of my hand, and holding it in front of her while leaping from cot to cot, and somehow reading it, shouted, "It's true, it's true." Flinging my letter on the window seat, she cried, "Read the other letter."

"This one is from London," I said, carefully opening the crackly pre-war cream envelope. "But it's not my mother's handwriting. Who else could have written to me?"

Certainly it was none of my relatives. They had forgotten me.

I read aloud the single matching sheet of cream paper inside:

"Cricklewood

London

May 9, 1945

Dear Miss Moss:

As you doubtless now know, we forwarded your letter on racism to Frank Robinson's New York address in America.

You sound like a very interesting young lady. My mother and I would like to invite you to tea next Sunday, at four in the afternoon. Please let me know by return post if you are able to come.

Yours truly,

Jonathan Goldstein,
Letters' Editor
Life Magazine"

He'd written it May 9th, the day after VE-Day and our street celebrations.

"The editor of *Life* has invited you to tea?!" Helga exclaimed. "What's a Letters' Editor? Is he important? Is the editor the same as the letters' editor?"

"I'm not sure," I said.

"Goldstein. That's a Jewish name," Selma said. "I bet his mother wants to look you over, to see whether you'd make him a good wife. What will you wear?"

"Oh, Selma, don't be ridiculous. He's just being kind. I'll wear my new dress."

With our clothes ration coupons, Mummy had bought me a beautiful new white dress; now I had two dresses. What luxury!

"As soon as I'm sixteen I'll marry my sweetheart and have babies, like my mother," Selma said.

Secretly, I envied her parents' love for each other and for Selma, since my family didn't miss me at all. But I chastised myself for envying her; she had not heard from her parents for six years. However, I was thrilled that the Editor and his mother wanted to meet me.

"Why would a letters' editor of a famous magazine ask a schoolgirl to tea?" Cookie sniffed.

"I'm 16," I said. "I'm a young woman. Besides, he says I sound interesting."

Cookie flipped a scarce rubber band stingingly at my face. I wanted to smack her.

"You *must* write and accept, today," Helga said, her enormous eyes serious.

I wrote immediately to the Letters' Editor to say that I would be delighted to come to tea on Sunday, and would take the train home to London next Friday. Since we had just won the war in Europe, British evacuees were now allowed to travel by train to visit their London families. Refugee travel was still restricted.

With the war in Europe finished, I needed only Nurse's permission to go home for the weekend. I'd stay with my parents and sleep on the kitchen couch, even if Mummy's friends sat on me, (she had rented my room to two Polish Free Fighters). I'd see my grandparents, aunt Mitzi, Uncle Sam, (Uncle Max was still a soldier in Egypt) and most important, on Sunday, I'd go to tea with the editor.

I boarded the train from Great Chesterford wearing instead of my stodgy daily school uniform, my only dress, a pretty blue, a bunch of fresh violets pinned at the throat.

As Yanks got off at Audley End, I leaned out of the window to breathe in the beautiful May air. A breeze riffled my brown, curly hair. An American officer walking along the platform looked up and said boldly, "Can I have one of your violets?"

I laughed, plucked one from the bunch, leaned down and gave it to him. As the train began slowly to move, he walked beside me, saluted, and said, "See you in Tokyo."

Suddenly, a dark cloud passed overhead. A shiver passed through my body. Something momentous was going to happen.

More Yanks boarded the train at Stanford, the other Yank air base en route to London to celebrate there the end of the war in Europe. Tommies and Yanks crowded into the corridors, singing and cheering, some drunkenly. I realized that the Yanks, too, like the Tommies, were looking forward to returning to their American homes and sweethearts after we had won the war against Japan.

Outside Liverpool Street Station in London everyone was dancing and singing, celebrating VE-Day in the streets. Although I had not seen my parents for two years and had written that I was coming home, no one met me. I walked the two miles to our East End house. The front door, as always, stood open. Mummy and Daddy sat in the kitchen drinking tea. "Hallo," I called out, entering the kitchen.

"Oh, I didn't know you were coming," Mummy said.

"I wrote to tell you I'm going to tea with Mr. Goldstein, the editor, on Sunday."

"I forgot. Dad and I are going to the Fleet Street peace celebration. Coming?"

"Of course."

What a silly question! Of course I wanted to celebrate peace, and with my parents. I had seen Mummy and Daddy only twice in six years, and then, not together.

"Take the camera, Alf," Mummy shouted to my deaf father.

We three clambered up the winding iron stairs of the red Number 6 bus going to the City of London. I loved riding on the top deck, looking down at everyone, and staring through the upstairs windows at those first story walls on which were carved wonderful white stone men's frowning faces, angry mouths wide open above curled stone beards; the open mouths forever silently shouted epithets at top deck bus riders like me.

As we drew near Fleet Street the bus driver called out, "All off. Can't go any further, too many crowds."

Buses stood marooned, empty, unable to move for the thousands of celebrants. In other buses, however, people trapped inside were unable to get off because of the mobs surrounding their exits. Crowds of people, exhausted from six years of nightly bombings, from demolished houses, civilian deaths, 200 killed a night, from anxiety about missing sons and lovers, from the sorrows of wounded and dead soldier relatives, the fears of Nazi invasion, rationing, and still unbelieving of peace, drifted, eyes dazed, dreamy, as if sleepwalking, instinctively heading herd-like, toward Buckingham Palace. On the way, British flags snapped in the breeze over Nelson's column, the walls pasted with signs reading, "Victory over Germany 1945." Other signs proclaimed, "*Annus Mirabilis*," The Year of Miracles, and "It's all over in the West." "Hurray for VE Day, hurray for Victory in Europe."

Pockets of people danced in the streets, squeezing aside only to let pass conveys of British and American trucks, into which girls laughingly climbed, kissing unshaven, grinning, soldiers.

Mummy, Daddy and I drifted with the massive crowds until we reached the tall, black iron railings of Buckingham Palace. The Royal Family and Churchill stood solemnly on its British-flag-draped balcony. The king and queen gravely waved, and Churchill, the British Bulldog, gave his famous V for Victory sign. The two Princesses sat there gracefully still and solemn. The crowd roared and waved British flags. The Royal Family, to me, descendants of conquering soldiers, was simply decorative. They did not excite me. My real excitement swirled like my new white dress, around the coming tea with the *Life Magazine* Letters' Editor: my reason for coming to London.

Sunday was the big day. Cricklewood, where the editor lived, was a posh North London neighborhood. I imagined the editor and his mother living in a beautiful house with shiny parquet floors, rich red oriental carpets, translucent china cups and a silver tea- pot. They'd serve watercress sandwiches, and if they hadn't used up their sugar ration, little cakes. Suppose they even served crumpets with clotted cream and strawberry jam?

I prepared for the visit by running hot water in our new bath. With the restitution money the government gave us for our bombed-out roof and windows, Mummy had halved my large bedroom and installed a bathroom. No more going to the Public Baths with Mummy. I felt a twinge of regret, since Mummy's and my pre-war Thursday visits to bathe together had been our one weekly moment of intimacy.

But I smiled excitedly as I dipped my toes in our new bath, and tested our first running hot water: our new post-war luxuries. The smelly, wooden lavatory still sat, newspaper for toilet paper, in the back yard. "He's in the Houses of Parliament," Mummy would tell a man who came for a shave and haircut. "Alf! Customer!" she'd scream.

Using up our last ration coupons, Mummy had bought me this beautiful white cotton dress. Wartime dresses, -- most of our fabrics went for soldiers' uniforms-- had been coarse, skimpy and colorless. This post-war dress, made of soft, rich cotton, had a design: a square neck, a tapered bodice which enhanced my slender waist, and a daringly flared skirt. When I had twisted in it, the whole skirt had whirled round me like a ballerina's. I had tried it on and admired myself in my new long bedroom mirror. The dress showed off to perfection my long throat, the firm rise of my young breasts, my new neat waist and great legs, now sheathed in black market silk stockings.

The soft whiteness of the dress accentuated my dark curls and green-gold, Tartar eyes. In this dress, I appeared transformed like magic into a beautiful young woman. Mr. Goldstein would love me in it. As I lovingly spread the new white dress out on my bed, I stroked the luxurious folds in the skirt. This was my first really grown-up dress.

After the bath and the sweet shower of snow-white talcum powder, I was putting on my brassiere and suspender belt, when Mummy walked into my bedroom. Glancing at the new dress spread elegantly on the bed she said, "Don't wear that. Wear your school uniform."

"But Mummy, this dress is beautiful. I want to dress like a young lady."

"No, wear your school uniform. He'll be an old man and think you darling."

"I wear that shapeless gym tunic and tie every day. Meeting an editor at *Life* is a special occasion."

I didn't say that the uniform hid my new beautiful sixteen-year-old figure, which Mummy refused to notice, and that the white dress showed me for the ripe young woman I was. I'd been too young to date the Yanks, and in any case, had only one blue dress, barely used because we wore the stodgy high school uniform every day.

"Surely now that I'm sixteen I can wear this dress to meet Mr. Goldstein," I said, looking longingly at the pretty white robe.

"Don't answer back, just do as I say," Mummy snapped, her face flushing, eyes darkening, her voice ominously lowered. Challenged, my mother would fly into such a violent rage, that my father and I avoided all arguments with her. Besides, British children were trained to obey parents. We were children until 21 and then became adults.

Never mind, I thought. The Editor had said I sounded interesting. I would visit him wearing the white dress at another time. Slowly, I put on the hateful school uniform, blouse, tie, gym tunic, the thick lisle stockings, heavy brogues, velour hat, and rode the underground to Cricklewood.

I found the house and rang the bell. Mummy had said he'd be an old man.

A tall handsome young man, with curly blond hair, bright blue eyes, wearing a Harris brown tweed suit and brown suede shoes, opened the front door. A joyous welcoming smile lit his face. Then he saw my school uniform.

"Oh!" he said, his smile fading. His face fell, as if someone had hit him. I knew immediately he'd expected that other, beautiful girl in the white dress.

"Here, I am, under here," I wanted to shout.

My face burned with anger at my mother making me look so childish, shame that the editor had spurned me, and chagrin that he showed so blatantly his disinterest in me.

"Come in," he said glumly. I followed, slouching behind his tweedy back.

I had hardly entered the house, and tea with the editor was already a disaster.

Inside, the living room was windowless and gloomy, the wooden ceiling so low I feared he would hit his head on it.

On a low couch sat a lady with a mass of auburn ringlets, her eyes dark and passionate as a gypsy's, wearing a décolleté velvet dress that exposed a milk-white throat. Warm amber beads glowed against her white skin.

"This is my mother," Jonathan Goldstein said in a monotone.

"What a pleasure to meet you," she said, extending her white hand like a queen's.

I felt she, at least, saw through the uniform to the real me. That didn't help.

"Do come and sit down next to me." She patted the cushion on the couch. "Excuse the disarray," she gaily waved at the vast, dark room, empty but for a few sticks of old furniture and cluttered dishes. "We're emigrating to America in two weeks. We thought we'd like to meet you before we leave. We are refugees from Hungary who had to leave everything to save our lives and escape. My poor husband was killed." Her eyes filled with tears. "We had such a good life there. Every luxury you could want, and now look at us." She waved a slender hand over the gloomy room, gave a deep, soulful sigh. "Ah well, we're lucky to get away with our lives, let's be happy."

Mummy told me, "Beware of Hungarians, Romanians and men in suede shoes."

I glanced at Hungarian Jonathan Goldstein's suede shoes, and then at the room.

Although the day outside sparkled, the room was so dark and so foggy I could barely see the end of it. Suddenly, I longed for the bright, sunny White House Big Girls' room in Great Chesterford. The old wooden floor in this house tilted down; I felt that at any moment,

Jonathan Goldstein, Mrs. Goldstein and I, along with the thick cheap china piled on the table ready to pack, would all slither to the floor, the china crashing into smithereens.

Beside the tilted couch and huge lopsided table, there was one chair. On the chair, like a fat cat, sat an old chrome electric toaster, its black wire like a cat's tail trailed along the floor, its end plugged into the wall. So this was what an electric toaster looked like. At home, a long tin toasting fork, onto which we stuck a thick slab of white bread, both held over a roaring coal fire, served as our toaster. London's East End was famed for its outdoor lavatories, bathless houses, and I'd never there seen an electric toaster.

A few colorful finger puppets lay strewn about the room. "This is how I earn a little money," my hostess sighed.

How could they afford to go to America? Probably HIAS, the Hebrew Immigration Aid Society must have given them money to go. No doubt the editor, himself a refugee, mainly supported his widowed mother. I had thought Cricklewood was a fancy area. If so, this must be the cheapest and ugliest house in Cricklewood.

The sole pretty item in the room was a gleaming silver toast rack, which shone through the gloom. Mrs. Goldstein rhythmically dropped slices of white bread in the toaster from which they popped up, brown, like magic. As she deftly removed the toast to the silver toast rack, she immediately popped two new slices of bread into the electric toaster. The second she set the toast between the silver bars of the toast rack, Jonathan Goldstein snatched up the slices, slathered jam on them and wolfed them. The editor was so quick, Mrs. Goldstein almost had to pry several pieces away from the toast rack to offer me before he reached them. Leaning forward, she offered me the slices of toast as if they were sumptuous gateaux instead of hot bread.

Usually, when invited to an English tea, the hostess served guests with dainty little sandwiches and all kind of cakes. Here, there was nothing to eat but toast, jam, and tea. I had traveled a long way; had not eaten before leaving, and felt the surge of a healthy sixteen-year-old appetite. So, apparently did my senior, Jonathan Goldstein, for he rapidly devoured about ten pieces of toast. After his cordial letter, I had expected a rousing discussion on racial equality, but since my appearance had so apparently disappointed him, he made absolutely no attempt at conversation. If he didn't like my looks, I thought resentfully, he could at least have tried to talk to me. A curse on my school uniform; I was ready to strip it off and show him my beautiful young body. And what about me being 'an interesting young lady'?

What happened to that part of me? He could have tried to find it. I felt so angry, that all my usual wit deserted me.

Jonathan's mother presided over the chipped brown china teapot as if it were chased silver, pouring tea from it with an elegant flick of her wrist.

"Milk? Sugar?" she asked, looking deep into my eyes, as if these were crucial questions.

My eyes strayed back to the elegant silver toast rack. In spite of the room's shabbiness, I guessed that this toast rack was one of the few belongings Mrs. Goldstein had managed to save from her former luxurious Hungarian life.

Jonathan sat silently chewing toast, staring into space. Perhaps besides being disappointed in me, his home and the sparse tea embarrassed him. Suppose I had worn the beautiful white dress? How would he have been then? All boyish charm, I bet. In his letter he'd said I sounded interesting. Maybe the whole idea had been his mother's and he didn't even want to see me. But his eyes had lit up with joy in the second he opened the door, and before he saw my hateful tie, gym tunic, brogues and school hat.

Mrs. Goldstein chatted incessantly and charmingly about nothing in particular. I think Selma had been right, that she saw me as a good match for her son. Perhaps he'd been going out with a *shiksa*, a gentile girl. I was a respectable, British, Jewish educated girl and against racism. To a refugee, whose husband had been murdered because he was Jewish, I may have appealed to her, more than to her son.

How I longed to talk about meeting the racist Yank on the train, about my friends in the hostel, our daily ride to high school, and the fascinating encounters we had with soldiers on the trains; about my pen-pal Frank Robinson, and America.

Where were the witty remarks that sprang to my lips on the trains when I rode with the Yanks? They always put me at ease. Imprisoned inside my uniform, watching silent Goldstein wolfing toast and jam, I longed to leave. But I still wished I had worn the white dress, and that he'd liked me.

"You must come and visit us if you come to America." Mrs. Goldstein said, as if I were due to hop over next week. Suddenly I was a schoolgirl, in dress and pocket, totally dependent on my mother and father, without a farthing of my own.

Where would I ever get the money to visit America?

"I'd love to," I said.

Mrs. Goldstein produced out of nowhere a white parchment card with her name and an American address printed on it in an elegant script. I saw this as a sign to say goodbye.

"Thank you," I said, but I didn't know how to extricate myself.

As tea with the editor tediously wore on, Jonathan Goldstein seemed, like Whistler's mother, to fade into the wallpaper. My mouth ached from smiling. I was sick of tea and toast. I wanted desperately to go home. When I finally, politely got away, all Jonathan Goldstein could manage was a faint, dismissive flick of the finger 'goodbye,' as if the effort exhausted him.

"Why did you make me wear that stupid school uniform?" I raged at Mummy when I returned home, risking a slap on my face. Children did not question parents.

"I thought he'd be a fat old fellow and would think you looked a treasure in it," she answered laughing, for the first time in my life explaining herself.

"He was young and handsome. He wanted to see an elegant young woman and I looked like a stupid shapeless schoolgirl. I *begged* you not to make me wear that uniform. I *begged* you to let me wear the white dress. The whole tea was a disaster."

For the first time in my life I showed Mummy my dramatic side, which had won me annual roles in school plays. Only now I was not acting.

I waited for Mummy to smack me for talking back, but for once she didn't.

"Well cheer up, the news is good. We've encircled Berlin and caught that anti-Semite, Pétain," Mummy said.

"Fat lot of good that does me, tea was a total fiasco," I muttered. "I'll never see him again."

I promised myself that Mummy would not domineer me when I came home for good after the Allied victory in Japan. I had been almost independent for six years. I was no longer a child. And I would go to America; I would meet Frank Robinson and Jonathan Goldstein and Mrs. Goldstein. We'd have tea, with their silver toast rack and a perfect china teapot. I'd dress in the white dress, silk stockings, high heels like the grown-up I was, and Jonathan Goldstein and Frank Robinson would find me absolutely fascinating.

The time to break from Mummy was now.

At that very moment, after telling Mummy Jonathan Goldstein would never see me again, my turning point began. The end of my childhood faded away, and the beginning of my life as a young woman began to unfurl, like a blossoming rose.

As Mummy walked out of the room, I whispered, "Goodbye, Mummy."

But she had told me that I couldn't legally leave home until I was 21. I was very patient, calm, in the face of her attempts to break my will to hers, but planned my escape. Friends supported my plan. While completing high school and college, I secretly applied for American emigration and won a post-graduate scholarship to Columbia University.

Soon I'd be free. My first stop into the world of freedom would be to visit Jonathan Goldstein and show him the real beautiful, clever young woman he'd disdained. Then, I would pursue my studies.

I'd gained the courage to break free from childhood into womanhood because of that disastrous tea with the editor.

I should thank Jonathan Goldstein, but I doubted I would.

M&Ms

~

Sharon E. Mortz

Her silent affirmations kept her from going completely insane. Had everyone had gone crazy? The dating scene was nothing like her youthful search for love among tumescent pubescence. The Internet had equalized the sexes and initiated a transformation in dating -- The manifest destiny of feminism. But had the dating pool changed from nefarious to noble simply because of equal opportunity?

She wondered if a woman in her fifth decade enter this new world order and retain the art of subtle seduction. This sublime quest stemmed from a very carnal observation: men weren't whistling at her anymore. She knew she had to try the new mode of dating: The Internet. She approached this adventure with an open mind and a positive attitude. She was a confident woman and didn't need to wait around for a male to make a move. She was intelligent, cute and witty. Could she find love? Was there life after divorce and raising children in San Francisco? She composed her bio, aiming for saucy but sensible. She was comforted by her new font of possibilities.

She, like every woman from the time of Nefertiti, knew that the initial attraction was physical. Males disrobe mentally and women evaluate the sensitivity and success potential. Egyptian charcoal and berries had evolved into Chanel and Clinique and she immersed in bubbles, dabbed perfume, exfoliated, massaged emollients, foamed emulsions, dangled baubles as if preparing to give her acceptance speech at the Oscars. She repeated affirmations into the mirror, "You are worthy, kind and intelligent. You deserve the best," while strategically applying makeup to look natural. Her goal: a balance between looking great but appearing to have put no effort into the process. You know, a pinch-of-the-cheeks-a-bit-of-gloss-and-a-toss-of-my-head-to-ruffle-the-hair effect. It was so much work that by the time her escort arrived and she could finally smile and move without fear of breaking a sweat, she melted in a heap of relief.

Initially her ads and surfing netted many and varied prospects. She had her share of dates consisting of polite, stiff dinners sprinkled with monosyllabic conversations more resembling interviews than dates. Who said dating was fun? This is boot camp. Women are a sisterhood -- they need to share wisdom and experience. she rehearse the art of chatting in matters mundane or moving, mindless or momentous as the occasion dictates or attentively listen with a wide smile affixed until her cheeks hurt, hoping she is flattering, fetching, and funny. Will she ever learn? Nevertheless, sometimes despite rehearsals and wine, silence smoothers the date like drizzly fog douses grass fire and she visualize the universal justification, "free dinner."

She channel-surfed through her recent dating experiences recalling scenes as colorful as new M&Ms. There were gaps, of course, when her interest drained like sand in an hourglass. One benefit: her dating experience had coalesced her composite mate, like a police sketch of the FBI's most wanted, she is closer to identifying desired characteristics, universal truths and rendezvous rules. She pushes pause and contemplates a few relationships, rules and observations.

First, the Number One rule is keep the initial meeting brief. Then, obviously, one isn't challenged to concoct excuses. She assumed this rule was universal but it still should be promulgated because if your paramour had traveled an hour he may be put off by the half-hour coffee date. Short dates alleviate other problems: i.e., sitting too long can be embarrassing if your joints stiffen and feet swell making quick movements impossible. Hiking should also be avoided as nature walks can elicit a sneeze and embarrassment and there is the fear of West Nile.

A universal observation is that men add at least an inch to their height if they are less than 6 foot – probably two inches. Similarly, women subtract 20 to 30 pounds from their weight. This has been going on for so many years that women can no longer divulge their correct weight because men have no idea what *real* women weigh. They think all women weight 118 so if you don't, be evasive. "Trim" is a sufficient description. Leave the number for them to guess.

She developed a useful time management technique to employ while searching for love. If it is obvious that an encounter is not going to work, do an errand, like Christmas shopping, with your date. Then you have completed a chore but haven't hurt anyone feelings by dumping him on sight. There is the risk that he will think you are trying to include him in your life and follow you like a tail-wagging puppy.

***

One of her early dates was "non-material" Carl who was shorter by a bit. She decided to give it a try and not be so shallow. He had a sad face that looked like his last five wives had two-timed him. He suggested McDonalds for lunch. McDonalds in San Francisco? Do they have a wine list? How about a visit to her OB-GYN too? Wouldn't that would be fun!?! But she thought, "Give him a chance." Maybe he is paying large amounts of alimony to all those ex-wives. They chatted amiably and he shyly asked her to dinner. She'd gone this far.

We decided to confirm later and then he asked, "Could we go Dutch?" Who is Dutch? Oh no. That was too much. She couldn't do short and too-financially-challenged-to-buy-one dinner. Unemployment or underemployment is something she avoided unless I'm dating an astronaut between moon landings. She had her fun with unemployment when she was married. Translation: "non-material" means no money.

***

Phil was a construction worker. She'd always been partial to blue-collar men and apparently she's not the only one. Now that the sensitive, well-groomed metroman is waning in popularity, the macho man is in even more demand.

Phil wore a hard hat throughout their first meeting. He thought it made him sexier and he -coupled that with a rehearsed body-builder's swagger. They met for a drink at the Sheraton that was being renovated under his guidance and as they sat down, he conspiratorially leaned in to tell her his work was dangerous. She thought that he would gallantly offer her a hard hat. She wondered if his work was so shoddy that the building was in danger of caving but she feigned awe at his manly profession. When he ordered a coke she considered starting a diatribe about the evils of sugary soft drinks and the salubrious benefits of the wine that she had ordered but held back. She considered changing her order but if the building was going to cave, one of them had to keep their cool and a glass of wine could help her keep mine. She was bareheaded and vulnerable.

Then he divulged that he was a member of AA. Aha – the coke. He pulled out his day planner and she surreptitiously peered at the large handwritten entries to see that he had meetings scheduled every day. He also had an overeater's anonymous meeting that evening but said he'd like to see her after that. She realized that she wouldn't fit into one of those little squares on his planner. One plus: she was able to help Phil crystallize *his* composite date too. Days later, she recognized his familiar ad on the Net with a new line added. "No blondes."

***

Ben was a self-employed electrician who lived in Half Moon Bay where he took her for a motorcycle ride to dine with his friends. She was the gyroscope providing navigational control in leveling the bike. When the cycle turned a corner, the pavement loomed inches away, she prayed, leaned the other way and wondered, "What is a 55 year old doing on a motorcycle?" He had a large extended family, deceased wife, business and they dozed through their dates. They were a perfect match but distance kept them apart and she never learned to lean into the turns.

***

I met John for mochas at the Polk Street Beanery and they hit it off conversing in fast forward. Their second mocha increased her jitters and their conversation sped into high gear causing her to dump the entire sweet, whipped-creamed elixir on his lap. He was barely fazed in his caffeine-altered state. He asked her to throw caution to the wind and take off with him for the weekend. If he had not talked her to death for hours about mowing his lawn, she might have considered the weekend assignation. He called her later and she promised to return the call but never did. His gardening stories were too exhausting.

***

Then she met the Satin Latin. He owned a bar, was smooth and urbane. He had a small scar above and through the upper portion of his lip, which added to his already significant sex appeal. He was perfect and glided when he walked. She knew there was a long list of broken hearts that preceded her and a longer list of them to follow. She did not care. She decided to keep it light and date this tanned heartthrob for fun.

She felt important when out with Satin so she jeopardized her health and looks by frequenting after-hours smoky bars with him. If exposed to smoke, her sinuses swell and her eyes turn into slits. He had the enviable quality of being a late sleeper while she never could sleep past 6:00 a.m. She had to resort to applying Lipton tea bags to reduce the swelling. In the evening's candlelight and smoke, she hoped Satin only saw the gossamer outline of her carefully made-up face. She considered puffy eyes a small price to pay and well worth being on the arm of the man that women were secretly hoping to encounter on the way to the ladies' room where they would press their phone number into his always dry, cool hand.

We went to her favorite restaurants -- Yabbies, Holy Grail, Antiqua and Tadich's – no fu fu with sculptures erected on their avant-garde dinnerware. One memorable evening, Satin whispered, "You look radiant tonight." The Lipton was working. She beamed and covered his hand with her manicured one. Their wine was followed by salad and cauliflower soup. As Satin elegantly spooned, his upper dentures imperceptibly fell into the soup. One moment his sparkling teeth were peeking out of his irresistible smile and the next, they were outlined in cauliflower. She was so stunned that she froze and could not utter a word of comfort. She was praying for another 7.1 Loma Prieta to divert attention from the moment. He was not perfect but with a smile and with the smoothness of the virgin olive oil creeping up the sour dough, he retrieved his dentures and reinserted.

***

Bill described himself over the phone and added his hair was getting "pretty thin on top." She had discovered another sensitive area for men. He was bald as an egg. Maybe he thought if he didn't mention it, no one would notice or he, chameleon-like, could regenerate a new thatch of hair with enough message and positive thinking. He was tall, good-looking and had a tough-guy quality that she found attractive. Maybe he was a bouncer or in the Mafia though I've never seen bald hit men. He always carried a wad of bills. Maybe he was an apprentice Mafiosi and put the squeeze on small liquor storeowners offering protection for money. Was that an entry-level position? He referenced his mother and his Catholicism characteristic of the morals of the Mafia. They cross themselves and genuflect before a hit.

We had a beer together and he suggested they go to his apartment. She was intrigued but somewhat afraid and declined, hoping I'd revealed the proper proportion of virtue. When he called again, and *again* he asked her to meet him in his neighborhood, near his apartment, he added that he was agoraphobic. What would he divulge next: that he's suicidal? She didn't want to be on the other end of the hot line so she said no. She didn't know if it was fear or if she was trying to tantalize him but she continued to say "no."

***

Les was an imposing, handsome man with ocean blue eyes who also rode a motorcycle and ate at Burger King exclusively, which had made him sick for years until he discovered that his body needed nutrients. He started taking Blue Klamath Algae and improved. They stumbled upon their mutual interest in nutrition and thought that tenuous bond meant they had something in common and they could find a connection around shopping for vitamins.

He contemplated starting his own limo business and, like a toddler putting together his first puzzle, was struggling with his intention and motivation. She appreciated his struggle and listened to his plans. He was yet another recovering alcoholic. Seems there are many Boomers struggling with addiction and I, like an eight ball, had scattered many colorful prospects. My radar bounced off them especially if they were on a motorcycle.

We went to movies, church and health stores together and had the beginning of a relationship. He spoke with relish about endless past relationships attempting to convince me, or maybe himself, that he was once a player and a catch. Better get in line now while the getting is good. His endless stories left her in a quandary: should she put him out of his misery and put her out of mine and she ended their involvement.

***

Then she met Jim. When he first called, his nervous laugh made her uncomfortable and she put him off twice. Was he an assassin sent by one of her scorned lovers to annihilate me? Luckily, he was persistent and the eve before her trip to Alaska, they went out for a drink. She used her time management technique and decided to meet him since she typically did not sleep the night before a flight and she would be imbibing *somewhere* to sedate the nerves.

Our prearranged rendezvous destination was the Bell Tower on Polk, and when he drove by she knew him from his description. He was drop-dead gorgeous, tall with sun-bleached hair pulled back in a ponytail. After their second date, they sat on her couch listening to music and talking when Jim reached over and kissed me. She knew that he was not going home that night. Jim was sweet and sexy.

He owned all kinds of animals and lived in a one-room edifice in Montara. The bathroom was the only separated room but he had tons of land and an ocean view. It was cute and functional and she grew to like it. We'd rent movies and sit in his bed watching them and ordering their favorite pizza: gourmet vegetarian with extra anchovies. Sometime he would make a coffee concoction for her with lots of sweetened condensed milk, which was to die for. He would joke, "That's what she like -- a girl who walks in and gets into bed." She had no choice. Not only was she compelled by Jim's allure but the bed was the only piece of furniture aside from kitchen appliances in his small apartment. Who wanted to sit on a toaster to watch TV and eat pizza?

The outside furniture was for watching the animals romp and the surf dance. She really liked Jim, and though not an animal lover, was willing to share the bed with Jim's dog. She was afraid that he would get rid of her if she banned the dog.

One evening they had placed their pizza order, she hopped on the bed to pick out the movie, and the worst date nightmare erupted. She flatulated. No, she farted. She was so humiliated that she prayed the world would open up and swallow me. She said nothing hoping he wouldn't notice knowing it was not something that could be ignored.

The floods of 1997 washed out Highway 101 creating havoc in commuter's lives and in her love life. Their dates dwindled in proportion to the increased rain. I'm not sure what part flatulence had in the demise of their relationship.

Dating reminds her of a summer carnival game - keep throwing the balls into the vicinity of the target -- eventually you may get lucky and hit the mark. Maybe it's time to flip the hourglass and try again.

Blink

~

Michael John Paul Pope

"Jeeze!" I saluted a quick flat hand to my brow covering a fierce hot jolt of sunlight that seemed to come from nowhere bending me over in agony, to allow my eyes a chance to cool as I heard several gunshots that seemed to come from just around the next sun splashed corner. I rose up, straight, still covering my squinted eyes as best I could with a too small hand to do the job and hurried to the corner only steps away. Why was the sun so torrid, I wondered as I stepped up my pace to the nearing corner where I thought I heard the blast of shots echo. Six…., maybe seven shots, I tried to recall. The relentless sun's rays burned my shoulders through the feeble white cloth of my dime-store sports shirt as I approached the brilliantly sunlit corner at a faster pace. Almost there I thought. The curb in sight, I rushed to the corner, both feet hitting the end of the sidewalk with slapping thuds. The tips of my sneakers hung over the edge of the gum-encrusted half-painted curb as I looked at the scene already played out, good and hard in front of me. Several people lay in the filthy, merciless gutter, their guts splayed out like tentacles reaching for a bit of extra life. I counted three helpless chumps in police chalk positions spread out in a tight little formation of death. What happened, I wondered. Why was the sun so relentless? I again shaded my disgusted brown eyes from the rays, trying to make sense of the scene. Three bloodied and limp limbed young men were dying right here right now! Why wasn't someone doing something? The sun spewed down onto my blinded eyes as a chill swept over me.

I tried to examine the pageant of death lying at my feet. My eyes caressed the young man's hot sun-baked body, his ear length thick greasy black hair hung over long lashes fluttering with despair. A smallish nose and perfectly shaped mouth puckered in the glare. He looked like he was freshly shaven a polished tan lit his lifeless body. A black Nike golf shirt and black light weight jeans covered a toned and muscled body. A wallet was falling from the pocket as a siren broke my attention to the young man. I looked around to see a large crowd growing and milling. I grabbed the well-worn black leather wallet just before it worked itself out of its safe keep. The sirens wailed closer.

The crowd grew angry and boisterous as they paced and thanked their gods it was not they in the gutter. I opened the young man's wallet. His driver's license plastic casing flashed in the sunlight as I manipulated it, impatiently trying to dim the glare. The reflection gone, the young man's picture came into focus...........I know him...............I know him..........I scanned the license for his name.............Manny   Canbridge...................Manny Can......bridge............425 Ban............................Sirens blasted around the corner. I snapped the wallet closed and looked up in a fog of recollection. My head spun with a crippling headache of images and voices calling me from the depths of some awful nightmare.

Doors slammed and brakes screamed. Police were giving orders. I threw the wallet back by the young man hitting him in the soft of his midsection. It landed with a plop in the dying man's blood. I looked up from my stupor. Across the intersection to the opposite side of the street, a man with a red shirt and gray slacks stood looking directly at me. I recognized him. The sun was in my eyes. *Get the goddamned sun out of my eyes*. I squinted.................and tried to see him. *Its him! That's him!* I pointed and screamed. *That's him!!!* I yelled again and ran towards the man, my feet barley able to keep pace with my outrage. The young man with the red shirt seemed to be surprised by my charge. His eyes widened with astonishment as he turned to run, keeping a steady eye on my advance and taking off running towards the screaming sun settling down over the desecrated horizon of the heat-abandoned street, his sneakers making a rhythmical cadence of defiance.

I ran hard and fast. The young man was a short block ahead. He turned to weigh my determination. I thought I saw him nod but had to be mistaken. I wiped the salted sweat from my eyes with the back of my forearm. I started to feel ill, weak. I was drained and confused. The young man in the red shirt appeared to be muscular and athletic. He was dark skinned but not black, Asian maybe. His hair was streaming, dark and unusually curly for an Asian, his features flat, one-dimensional. He turned again and flashed a devilish smile. I wiped my brow again and tried to keep pace.

The young man started to pull away as I lost my initiative and determination to follow but did so anyway. I took a quick glance behind me to see if anyone else had taken up the chase... They had not. The young man in the red shirt took a corner looking over his shoulder as he disappeared around a thicket of hedges blocking meddlesome eyes from stealing the privacy of the family in the corner house. I struggled to keep up but persisted, knowing it was the right thing to do. I turned the corner and stopped. The young man was gone. I trotted along the narrow alleyway presumptuously called a street. It was where folks put out their garbage and kids played in the mud. It was not really used for vehicle traffic. My trot slowed to a brisk walk as I looked from right to left, one back yard to another trying to see something relevant. I could not and kicked the dusty dirt road in disgust.

I stopped at the next corner, a deserted meager intersection connecting the alley to a side street. The sun was beating down on my cold shoulders as I tried to cut through the fierceness of the sunlight with my red and swollen eyes and the humiliation of a mocking ghetto. I crept to the edge of the sidewalk, panning the street, then the alley, but I could not determine anything and could not see anyone. He was gone!

Giving up the chase but still wanting to find the young man in the red shirt I walked another block west along the deserted side street. It led to another alleyway, then another. I walked another block west for no good reason, down the adjacent alley and out the other side to another seldom used side-road, roaches scurried under my feet at the gutters edge defying me to step down into the blackness they called home. I stopped again and scratched my scalp, my hair drenched with spoil and decay. A giant horse fly buzzed my nose. I swatted it to the ground and watched it as it tried to right itself, buzzing and flopping around on the excrement encrusted walkway. I studied it for several seconds and then crushed it under the thin-soled layer of my sneaker where I felt its wings flutter and surrender to me. I panned the area again, looking to do the same to the young man, but no one stirred. Only the rats, again...scurrying the crooks and crannies of the alleyway looking for scraps from the dark back windows of a greasy kitchen. I turned and started back.

I knew the sun led me in the right direction. Back from the scene of death and carnage that led me to this spot I darken with a crooked shadow. I had to see what had happened to the young man in black but wondered if this was the alleyway that led from that corner of death. I turned another corner still looking unfamiliar to me and then turned another, and another. The houses looked more distressed, penurious. The sun was not as bright but still burned my slumping shoulders. Clouds seemed to gather over my head as the sky turned its back on the neighborhood. I stopped short and ducked behind a large and overgrown bush fighting with a backyard fence for superiority.

Across the alley at the back side of an adjacent crumbling house a young man sat smoking a cigarette with several other young and dangerous looking fellows. The young man was animated and obstreperous, flailing his arms and making sounds of gunfire with his rubbery mouth. It was he. The red shirt clinging to his greasy skin.

I protected myself as best I could from the muted light of an overcast and threatening sky, my white sports shirt and white summer jeans not providing me the best of camouflage as I watched the young man in red tell his tale of deceit and mayhem. After an hour or two of filling his four unsavory looking accomplices with his tale of phony contentment, the young man flicked his final butt and withdrew into the ramshackle house. His artful dodgers… close in tow. A lurking figure moved behind the crumbling screen door as the pack of thugs stepped inside their lair.

I skulked out the back of the alleyway trying not to be seen by man nor beast, hoping to return after dark to see… what I could see. After cruising the gutters for some nourishment and to fill my lungs again with life, I returned to the alley, behind the bush at the base of the white paint peeled picket fence, awaiting the young man in red. As I slumped behind my protective bush, my mind wandered, filling me with images of my life so far and those who were important to my careless development. I mused about the opportunities I squandered and chances I so arrogantly refused, the pure pleasure of tossing a ball and the scouts that wanted to give me blank checks to fill with ink. Never having said goodbye to either of my parents on their separate beds of death because the monkeys of Satan called……..and I so willingly jumped to fill my blood with euphoria. I fell into a not so pleasant sleep, my minds eye filled with disappointment and dread. I felt someone cradle the back of my head and lift it ever so gently. Then I awoke, expecting the young man in red to emerge for a night of carnage and knew he would not leave until he did so. He did not disappoint! Appearing out of the darkness of his burrow, he was quickly enveloped into the darkness of the night… turning to the insistent light of morning. The beast and his little fiends strode out the squealing screen door half eaten away by the insects it had intended to bar, swinging back with a hollow smack to the termite ravaged jam, they strutted down the garbage strewn stairs of the lair moving cautiously but arrogantly towards the dust coated alleyway.

The same red shirt so aptly draping the young man's blood gorged torso, looked fresh in the early morning's muddy haze. He was like the red beacon of hell leading all his collaborators dressed in crime black. Black… on black… on black is the night. The doers of no-good passed through the humid blackness like nocturnal chimeras, preying on whoever crossed their paths.

I cowered behind the large overgrown back-alley bush as the hoard of predators prowled the early morning dim and walked past me with the disdain I would have expected had they known of my presence. I smelled cheap cologne and cigarettes as the packs' scent wafted over the scum-covered leaves of the bush permeating them with loathe, tickling my nose with menace.

The darkest of nights passed its torch to the most foreboding of mornings I could ever recall as I waited for the pack to move to the periphery of eyeshot before I moved safely from behind my beloved bush. I stood peering down the alley like a rat in the safety of its natty sewer home. The voices of the pack disturbed the calm as they cursed the morning and swore at the night, they continued down the dusty alleyway headed to deeds........ unknown. I moved slowly behind, collecting maggots and destruction on the bottoms of my sneakers as I made my way down the garbage-perfumed alley.

It seemed like the day would never end as I continued behind the pack, staying in the shadows and out of the prying eyes of the cool absconding moon. The pack was on the move and it definitely had an agenda as they broke free of their home turf and moved through several neighborhood boundaries, walking with the confidence and assuredness of a highly trained military crew. The homes grew larger as we moved west, all the time remaining at the periphery of all major roads and commercial establishments. The pack was on a mission and hell was to pay.

I saw the pack make a sharp right down an oak-lined street of yet larger homes and more expensive cars. The pack seemed to quiet, moving more stealthily as the determined group of miscreants tiptoed deeper and deeper into the realm of the wealthy. I stayed as close as I could without being detected on the opposite side of the street and several hundred feet behind. The huge oaks that stood guard at the head of every enormous property blocked the early morning sun from giving me away and hid the pack from its evil intent.

I stopped behind one of the massive oak tree trunks and watched the pack as they hid amongst some hedges surrounding the front lawn of one of the bigger homes. I could not hear, but I saw the young Asian man I chased to his lair pointing and giving direction. The pack split up, each going to a different spot around the huge Italian-style home. I moved closer to the pack, picking a spot on the property directly across the street and watched them move closer to the mansion and its expansive Roman windows.

I watched with as much interest as I could muster considering I was feeling more uncomfortable with each passing minute. My head was spinning and my shoulders felt sore, my body weak. Although I had already slept, I felt like I still needed a good night's rest and hoped it would come soon. My mind must have been playing tricks on me as I watched the pack ply their trade to the unsuspecting family that lived in the giant home. I saw shadows without a body to cast them. Dark shadows moved through the immaculate landscaping and around the perimeter of the house. I shook my head to clear my thinking and focus my thoughts. But the shadows would not go away. It was like another pack of shadow miscreants were targeting the same house as the pack I had followed, but I knew this could not be and tried to concentrate on the business before me.

Just as the pack looked like they were moving too close to the windows of the house I saw a flashing light pounding off the oak trucks and the huge silent homes as the light worked its way up the street from the opposite side of the pack's approach from the east. I had to duck down and away from the light as it pulsed my eyes. I hoped the pack did not see me as I sat on the cool of the plush lawn, waiting for the lights to pull me to safety and deliver me unscathed, but they only grew stronger. I rose to my knees just as a police cruiser stopped in front of the huge stone-walled home and shown its hand directed spotlight on the beautiful house and gardens. The police cruiser then started moving slowly down the tree covered street, flashing its spotlight down every driveway as it crept away from purpose.

The flashing lights dimmed to a flicker as the morning sun peeked over the horizon, casting a promising haze on the privileged block. I glanced quickly across the street before surrendering my investigation on the young man in the red shirt when I saw the pack coming together from the periphery of the perfect estate like leeches to the scent of fresh flesh. They slithered together, gathering briefly on the front lawn of the magnificent property then quickly hunched over and ran to the back of the house. I watched from my protected perch as the miscreants disappeared behind the behemoth house and waited for the pack's plan to reveal itself.

Thirty minutes later, morning well underway, I heard the whine of a garage door opening but could not determine from where the sound emanated when a gleaming black Mercedes pulled from around the side of the estate across the street, making its way down the long driveway and then slowly turned west down the quiet of the street, leaves crunching under its polished tires. I knew I would not be able to follow, especially feeling as I did, but dashed across the well-manicured lawns just the same, behind the Mercedes, which was lengthening its lead.

Pumping my legs was exhilarating, thinking back to my days as a favored athlete and promising collegian as I followed the glimmer off the brilliance of the polished black car as it made its way down the tree-lined block. It turned left down what looked like a wider boulevard with heavier traffic. I rushed to the corner, looking south down the boulevard just able to catch a glimpse of the black Mercedes speeding away. A bus brushed past me, almost knocking me backwards, its obnoxious smell of diesel fumes and deafening engine roar cleared the cobwebs, collecting my thoughts for dispatch. I regained my presence and jumped through the welcoming doors of the growling boulevard line bus and slapped two bucks into the driver's indifferent hand as he sped away, knocking me backward into a waiting seat adjacent the burly driver. I looked out the ample front window of the speeding pollution spew'er for the Mercedes but was unable to spot it. Urine crept up my nostrils as I inspected my fellow passengers spread around the bucking bus like a spattering of bacteria waiting for an open wound. I scanned my arms and hands nervously.

The sun made its way over the yawning town slowly and deliberately, trying to break through the smog that encompassed us in a bubble of airborne scum. We sped down the boulevard, the Mercedes nowhere in sight. I felt dejected and anemic. My head lolled on my chest in self-pity. I looked up at the Mexican driver and then out the bird gifted windshield to measure my next stop when the black gleam of the Mercedes tweaked my eye. Sitting right their... dead ahead, tail lights blazing, exhaust--breathing by the side of the road like it had been waiting for me all along. I plucked the "Please stop!" pull wire to the grateful plunking sound of the bell. The corpulent Mexican bus-driver skillfully pulled the belching street-behemoth to within an inch of the curb. Its doors coughed open, and I oozed out onto the sidewalk, hoping any infestation remained behind and ran to a still closed corridor of an expensive-looking jewelry boutique just an earshot from the black Mercedes and waited for movement.

Another expensive gas-guzzler pulled up behind the Mercedes and turned off its haughtily purring motor. A well dressed stuffed shirt squeaked out of the luxurious silver car, grabbed a briefcase from the tiny sneering trunk, and walked towards and past me like I were mold spreading on a seldom seen wall. He fumbled with several locks and alarms and then entered his boutique to start another prosperous day. I turned back to the Mercedes. The snobbish looking boutique owner returned with some change he put in my palm and told me to please use another doorway. I looked at the change in my hand and nodded to the pig in fine dress. He answered his cell phone and walked back to his inventory of sparkling wares his pristine sneer awash in the green glow of his phone.

The sidewalks slowly filled, the traffic backed up, and I waited for a sign.

Nothing……….. I must have missed something. They must have parked and gone somewhere else. I did not know but felt they were still in the vicinity. I waited. The late morning sun heated up the corridor. I watched the gum and spittle melt on the griddle hot concrete, making its way down to the gutter when several people materialized from the imposing building next door to the boutique. They moved as a unit and I recognized the young man in the red shirt amongst the unit moving towards the Mercedes. It was most of the pack sans one surrounding a tall slender gentleman carrying two briefcases. He looked worried. The pack looked nervous. Amidst the pack was a shadowy figure I could not place. It was not a person but a shadow. It was not a shadow but an empty space, a vacuum of humanity darkened by the emptiness of its worth. I tried to understand what it wanted, this shadow. But I could not, instead refocusing my attention to the pack of miscreants and their evil doings as they pushed the well-dressed gentleman into the back seat of the fine automobile. The young man with the red shirt slammed down next to the gentleman while the other two ran to either side of the Mercedes, tearing away in a screeching storm of dust, rubber and depravity.

I ran to the curbside, not knowing what to do next and looked back at the building from where the pack with its gentleman in hand had emerged. First City Bank and Trust. And I knew what the pack had done. I looked for help, but no one cared. I waved down a bus that had not yet arrived and then hailed a speeding cab that jammed on its brakes, whizzing ten feet past me to a smoky stop. I noticed a woman running from the other side of the wide boulevard her heels clicking a message of authority and tried to beat her as I watched the Mercedes race from sight. We both hit the cab at the same time, opening our doors simultaneously and piled into the stinking yellow cab. We screamed out our destination as I tried to follow the Mercedes over the horizon. I told the woman my emergency as the cabby looked back at me with confusion but sped off down the boulevard. The well-heeled woman looked peripherally at me, disdain dripping from her glossed lips and disgust keeping her Coach bag close to her bosom, her white knuckles gripping the handle tightly.

She ordered the cabbie over at the next corner as we tore down the boulevard, closing in on the Mercedes. I was powerless as the Mayan-looking cabbie skidded for the curb. The haute socialite threw a crisp twenty dollar bill in my lap and slammed closed the cab door. *Go! I screamed. After the black Mercedes!* The Maya plastered the accelerator to the rotting carpet of the filthy cab floor and nailed my head to the seat-back. I smiled, feeling weaker and colder. My hand felt for a stream of air coming from the registers on the dusty dashboard of the Maya's cab but could not feel a thing. I rolled my shoulder to ease the pain but only exacerbated it.

We raced down the boulevard as I tried to locate the Mercedes. The world through the grunge-encrusted windshield became blurry and indistinct. But suddenly.........several blocks ahead.........I pointed..........*There! There it is! Go......Go! The Mercedes! On your left........Do you see it?* The Mayan checked me, and then the boulevard ahead.

"Si," He answered and stepped on it.

The blackness of the Mercedes was not clear to me. It appeared as though I were looking at it through a seldom-cleaned fishbowl. We approached fast, moving up to the rear of the German status symbol with the urgency of a killer tornado. Three doors of the Mercedes swung open as we stormed up behind it. The Mayan slammed the brakes... turned and flashed a gapped tooth wide smile waiting for praise. I threw the socialite's fresh twenty, added a crumpled twenty and a nod, and flew out the door into a chaotic swarm of traffic. The Mayan took off, leaving me stranded in the middle of the boulevard as convertibles looking for the beach and sedans racing to the suburbs swished past me. I made my way to the curb as the young man in the red shirt bolted out the rear street-side door, rounded the corner carrying a leather briefcase, and bounded down the sidewalk. Then another pack member shot out of the curbside rear door and followed behind the young Asian. The last pack member followed. Long shadows trailed the three thugs as they ran from the Mercedes and down the adjacent block leaving the doors of the car wide open for inspection.

I advanced towards the open doors of the Mercedes with caution, not being absolutely sure if the entire pack vacated the vehicle or not, what they were up to or what they had achieved. Several other curious pedestrians slowed their pace as they passed the open doors of the car, reacting in repulsed horror, stopping momentarily but then continuing their superficial lives, solaced that it was not they. I crept up on the open rear door as another indifferent, good Samaritan peered in from the other side. My eyes swelled as I beheld the scene stretched out on the rear black posh leather seat. It was the tall lean well-dressed businessman, and he was dead! Contorted into an appalling pose of dread and fear for the world to see and shake their heads with pity and scorn.

The well-dressed man was missing most of his head, blown off by a too powerful weapon.....too close to use. He represented that which was too rich to die and much too young to remember, too content to sympathize and too worthy to ignore. The father of four privileged bricks off the wall of power and prestige and a loving bottle blond trophy wife was now lying in the back seat of their super-car parked in the repellent gutter they so dutifully tried to avoid. Soon they would have to identify the loving provider by what remains to be recognized, a ring, a watch, the shape of his right earlobe. It had been taken for that which he woke and dreamed...............money! It was then I realized that the pack must have left one of their repugnant members back at the businessman's home for safekeeping. I did not know if I felt sorry for the dead man and his family as I stood peering in from the deep of the gutter, but I did feel envy for the softness of the seat he filled.

I held onto the open door of the dead man's Mercedes, thinking about who would be the lucky recipient of the elegant car. Just a pool of fermenting blood to soak up on the back seat, nothing to deter the status conscience. Drying blood congealed on my fingertips as I drew my sticking fingers from the rear door. I wiped the dead man's blood on my white trousers as sirens wailed up from the other end of the packed boulevard, screaming toward the "certain to lead" story of the night's evening news. I took one last look at the almost headless yet once pillar of the community and ran after the pack of murderous hellhounds.

I bounded down the sidewalk in pursuit of the young man in red and his band of renounced youths, the relentless sun having its way with me as it stripped me of any life I had left. I was running on fumes as I tore down the quiet street of cookie cutter houses and Japanese cars. The pack was a couple of blocks ahead, but I ran flat out in pursuit. I could hear their foot falls echoing throughout the neighborhood like firecrackers on the Fourth of July. Impressed with my stamina, which never served me in the past, I was actually able to make up ground on the pack, my steps ratcheted up to an Olympian pace as I took yard wide strides. The pack, only a block ahead, turned to see who it was that dared to follow them. Shadows mixed with the pack as they stampeded down the unsuspecting block. My head felt disembodied, floating several feet above me as I raced towards the pack and its shadow hunters. I knew I was close to losing consciousness but also knew it was too late to give up. I convinced myself that I was the only one who was onto their murderous crime spree and that I must see this thing through or live with the consequences of my guilt.

I ran harder, focusing on my strides, letting each footfall mark a hypnotic cadence that kept me awake. Whap..whap..whap..whap..whap..whap.... tolled each slap to the hot cement as they echoed off each house I swept past. The sun reached down and scratched at my eyes as I tried to focus on the task ahead. I squinted in defiance of Apollo and his daggers of fire and continued forward, closer to the pack. The dogged roasting sunshine cut into my flesh. It consumed me. Eating at my last drop of energy, I was forced to pull up for a short respite. My hands dropped to my bended knees, holding me from collapsing onto the sun-baked walk. My breathing... shallow, and arduous, as I watched my chest fill and collapse. I straightened up after only a minute or two, looking ahead to the pack. I struggled to cut through the glare and heat striations coming off the baking concrete as I looked in desperation for the pack. They were gone.

I advanced again, slowly, one foot and then the other. I knew I hadn't long but did not know why or what exactly I was telling myself. One more step, then another...........I stopped and took inventory of the area. It............it looked familiar.........I somehow...............I've seen this place. Another step.......... A gunshot.........up ahead. I looked through the fire of heat and wall of unrelenting light leading straight down the walk to the near but distant corner. I ran...........the sun heating my exhausted and failing body as I pushed ahead. The curb in sight, I rushed for it, both feet hitting the end of the sidewalk with slapping thuds. The tips of my sneakers hanging over the edge of the gum-encrusted half painted curb as I looked at the scene playing out in front of me. What..... I thought,

Bullets whizzed through the air as I balanced on the edge of the curb like a reluctant Acapulco rock diver looking at shallow surf below. The red shirted Asian man was backing away from the scene, facing directly at me, his gun blazing at the young man in black standing between the both of us. Two of the thugs also dressed in black were firing directly at the young man in black standing before me, he did not seem to have a weapon and looked surprised by the turn of events. The two thugs also seemed surprised when they took fire from the young man in red who held both brief cases, one under his arm and one clenched tightly in his fist as he fired away at all his accomplices until each one lay dying or dead. Sinuous penumbras darted between the pack, twining amongst the three gun-toters as they fired at each other and particularly at the young man standing several yards in front of me. I felt like I should be ducking for cover but for some reason could not. I was rooted like one of the tall palms that lined many of the streets like righteous sentinels, unable to take a single step. My arms hung stiffly off my shoulders, palms facing front like I was about to receive a blessing in the form a hot determined round.

 The blood drained from my head like an unplugged sink. Chill nuzzled me, beckoning me from beyond my prospective. The piercing sun dropped me to my knees. I watched the young man in the red shirt back away to the adjacent corner, leaving the remaining pack floating on the blistering asphalt like driftwood swept up from an angry sea readying to spit them into the sewer at the mouth of the corner. I convulsed, and then bowed to the gods of regret. Blood oozed from the two young atrocities cradled by the filthy gutter. A third but undefined image was evident, but I could not focus clearly as I rubbed my eyes for sympathy. I waited for a signal while lights flickered around the periphery of my cognizance reminding me of the police cruisers lights by the tall well dressed man's home earlier that morning.

 My knees started to ache as I looked up to an impending sky. My arms rose with up-turned palms. The chill now pervasive, I gazed out over the dying pack. The sun shielded my eyes from harm as my will surrendered to retribution. I noticed the young Asian man still standing on the adjacent corner looking over his accomplishment and scowling at the friends he betrayed, and knowing that I was meant to be betrayed as well. Anyone would do the same given the opportunity, I thought as I bled into the white-hot street. I noticed an undefined image lying in the gutter start to rise like a malignant growth from the blackness of the asphalt. The droopy black phantasm gathered from the black outline in the gutter, inflating like an evil swell of doom, a head grew from the growing mass of darkness drooping onto its chest as it matured into a viable presence.

 I watched as the thing stood, got its bearings and then race towards me with a determined intent. I covered my face in anticipation of a collision as I felt the blackness envelope me. I heard a consoling squishing sound and was released from the prison of immobility, looking up at the boundless heavens, the blackness draining like scum from the depths of a cesspit as I floated toward the young man in black swimming in blood. My eyes were slits, inhibiting my vision of the uniformed man at the end of the gurney pushing me across the steaming asphalt, a large crowd gathered around looking on at the carnage at their feet. I felt a jounce, the muted sky gone replaced by the florescent lights of an emergency vehicle. A soft nurturing black woman dressed in a white paramedics uniform sat beside me, taking my blood pressure. I saw her lips move and knew she was speaking to me, but I could not determine what see was saying. My eyes closed more tightly. I heard her say, "You're going to be all right, Manny," but knew she was lying. I felt her hand slip behind my blood soaked head as she cradled it in her nurturing hand, lifting it from the gurney. My eyes closed more tightly and tighter still. I saw little, then nothing, forever.

The End

MIXED PRAYERS

Randy Susan Meyers

I. Maddy

I never knew what kind of mood Ben would be in at breakfast. Each day I spun the wheel on the Ben chart, hoping the arrow would hit happy-husband, or at the very least, neutral-guy. This morning he landed on total-bastard, holding me personally responsible for Caleb's tantrum which—oh, horror!—had cost him twenty minutes of work.

"Maddy, you have to learn to say no to Caleb," he'd said. "He's almost seven. He needs to learn control." Ben banged his briefcase on the hall table, snapped it open, and jammed in the *Boston Globe.*

Right, Ben. However, he was crying because I said he couldn't take his turtle to camp. Isn't that saying no? Oh, and by the way, could you stop slamming things?

I didn't say that. I held my tongue by counting parquet floor tiles in the hall and instead said, "The kids are waiting in the car."

"They can wait another minute," he'd said. They don't always have to be number one, damn it. See, you're just making my point, Maddy."

I didn't have a clue what his point what was; but on the other hand, I didn't care much either. "Right, Ben."

What an all-purpose word *right* had become in our family. Had it become our polite way of saying *I am acknowledging you have spoken, but am choosing not to engage in any meaningful way?* Lately, I found myself using it all too often.

Caleb should be reading better. His teacher is an idiot.
Right, Ben.
Your mother spoils the kids.
Right, Ben.

"Right, Ben," I repeated. My need to be behind the wheel of my car was stronger than any desire to prove a point. I grabbed an umbrella, thrust it at him, and we went to work.

\#

It was five-thirty; I was home from work and in the mood for nothing so much as a chemical vacation. I touched my tongue to my teeth, imagining the bitter taste of a half-tablet crumbling in my mouth, but the rites of family happiness demanded my attention.

I needed to make dinner. I needed to call my mother, pay the mortgage, and clean two toilets. I needed to find a stamp and give my children feelings of self-worth. And since Ben and I had fought that morning, I should do something to soothe him—fellatio came to mind.

Gracie and Caleb sprawled next to the couch where I'd collapsed, recovering from their day at camp: Caleb, half-asleep, rubbing his cheek with his thumb, Gracie's glazed eyes fixed on the television. Pressing the small of my back, I tried to ease the permanent muscle knot lodged there. My stomach growled. Cooking held as much interest as grinding glass into my eyes.

Fish sticks?

The back door slammed open. My older daughter banged her backpack on the kitchen table.   "Hannah?" I called.

"*What?*"

I struggled up from the couch and went to the kitchen. "I just wanted to make sure it was you." I loathed my tentative tone.

"Were you expecting anyone else?" she asked.

"It could have been Daddy."

"Right." Hannah looked at the clock and lifted her eyebrows.

Newspapers we'd tried to read at breakfast covered half the table. Hannah stared into the refrigerator as I gathered the papers, unsure whether to put them in the recycle bin or not. Had Ben finished them?

"There's nothing to eat," Hannah said. "In Caro's house—"

Before I found out just how superior a shopper Caro's mother was, Gracie's scream interrupted us.

"Mom!" she yelled.

Hannah followed as I hurried towards the living room.

Blood leaked from Caleb's hand. Shards of glass surrounded him, droplets of milk clinging to the pieces.

"What happened, Gracie?" I knelt next to a sobbing Caleb and took his hand.

Gracie's mouth trembled. "I just got up, that's all, and I knocked over his milk glass. Then he got mad and threw it, and then he broke it, and then he tried to pick it up, and then he cut himself." She scrambled over, handing me a wadded-up napkin. "It wasn't my fault."

"It's okay, baby." I pressed the napkin against Caleb's hand.

"Hannah, get me a damp towel."

Blood soaked the napkin, dissolving the paper as I exerted pressure.

"Make it stop, Mommy!" Tears cut through the dirt on Caleb's cheeks.

I pressed down firmer on the napkin. Gracie mopped up the spilled milk with a dirty tee shirt from her backpack.

I pressed the hem of my black cotton skirt over the napkin before blood ran onto the carpet. Hannah handed me a damp towel, then twirled the bottom of her long brown braid as she watched us.

"I'm going to check on the bleeding," I warned Caleb. He squinted as I looked under the towel. "It looks okay, hon. I'm going to wash it out."

"No! It'll hurt." He tried to pull his hand away, but I held him firmly.

Hannah knelt next to us. "Tell you what, C. You let Mom wash out the cut, and after I'll play Monopoly with you."

Caleb's smile came through like a sun shower.

"That's sweet, Hannah," I said. "Thank you, hon."

"Can I play?" Gracie asked.

"No," said Caleb. "Just me and Hannah."

Gracie's lip got that quivery look that made me feel torn between soothing and slapping. She performed the tiny signature genuflection she'd picked up from Ben's mother, a woman given to crossing herself reflexively. Gracie's gesture unsettled me. I should buy her a Jewish star or maybe some Unitarian symbol, if such a thing existed, before Grandma Frances hung a crucifix over Gracie's bed. Mixed marriage only went so far.

"Monopoly is better with more people," I told Caleb.

"No. I just want to play with Hannah."

Gracie pulled at her camp-grimy toes. "How about you and I make chocolate sauce while they play?" I suggested. "How about hot fudge sundaes for supper?"

Gracie raised her chin off her knees. "Really? Ice cream for supper?"

I pushed back her sweaty black curls, the only visible part of me she'd inherited. "Why not?"

#

A child leaned on either shoulder. My feet were propped on the coffee table as I bobbed in and out of sleep. Dirty bowls decorated with blobs of hardened fudge littered the room. We stirred at the sound effects of Ben's nightly return. Scrape of heat-swollen door opening.

Keys dropping on the hall table. Briefcase thudding on the oak floor. Shuffling of letters and magazines as he sorted through the mail. Sighs of relief or disgust indicated whether I should be on the alert. It all seemed audibly benign, or at least in the neutral zone. Thank God. It might be a Swiss night.

Ben walked in and looked at our collapsed bodies and the scattered pieces from the abandoned Monopoly game. Gracie pulled away from me and ran to him, throwing her hands around his waist. He stroked her black ringlets into a little bundle at the back of her head as she leaned into his softening middle.

"It looks like a war zone in here," he said. "What happened?"

"We had some excitement," I said. "Caleb cut his hand on a broken glass." Caleb held out his bandage-swathed hand, his eyes fixed on the television.

"You okay, cowboy?" Ben asked. He gave Gracie one last pat and walked over to the couch. "Does it hurt?"

Caleb shrugged. He looked at me as though seeking the right answer.

"How did it happen?" Ben tugged on his chin—his poker-tell. Steam was building. I leaned over and kissed him, hitting the side of his mouth he offered. "Forgetting anything?" I asked. "Hello, Maddy? How are you?"

He exhaled. "Don't start. I've had a rough day. What happened?"

"He rolled over while he was sleeping and cut himself on some glass," I lied.

"Where was he sleeping? The recycle bin?"

"Very funny. A glass broke. End of story." There. I'd snuck in the truth.

"Jesus, Maddy, can the kids eat and drink at the table like normal people?"

Caleb rubbed his good thumb back and forth across his knee. Gracie crossed herself.

"Not now," I said. "Please."

Ben flexed his shoulders, leaned back on the couch, and stared at the ceiling.

"We had ice cream for supper, Dad," Caleb announced.

Hannah's shoulders squared. Gracie pressed into me.

Ben turned to Caleb. "Ice cream?"

"With hot fudge," Caleb added.

"Nice to be rewarded for breaking a glass, huh?" Ben kicked off his shoes and raised his eyebrows, looking over his glasses at me.

"Since I haven't fallen or broken anything, what do I get for supper?"

Hannah jumped up. "Why don't I make you eggs, Dad?"

"That would be terrific. You have no idea." He leaned back and closed his eyes, pushing off his shoes with the balls of his feet.

Gracie came over and tapped his forehead. He opened his eyes and gave her a tired smile. "What is it, cupcake?"

"Want me to cut up carrots for you?"

I grabbed the laundry basket and hurried out.

After throwing in a white wash, I looked through the crowded shelves until I found the fabric softener. Then I dragged over a small dusty stepstool and climbed up, stretching until I could feel behind the jumble of cleaning supplies. Where was it? I swept my hand back and forth, reaching further and further. *Please, God.*

Finally, I pulled out a small baggie holding a few tablets. I took out a yellow one, slivered off a quarter, and swallowed it dry.

II. Ben

Half way to dropping Hannah off at camp, Ben remembered the meeting papers, picturing them right where he'd left them on the bed. He'd have to go back home after before going to his meeting. And it was starting to rain. Son of a bitch.

Hannah flipped the car locks on and off as he raced to make an amber light, placing her hand on the door handle as he pulled up to the camp entrance.

"Wait till I stop," Ben said. "Are you trying to kill yourself?"

"I know you're in a really big rush, Dad."

"Lose the attitude. I got you here on time, didn't I?"

"Thanks so much, Daddy."

Ben ignored Hannah's treacle-sweet tone. "You're welcome. Have a good day."

Carefully shutting the door, *no slamming, see Mom,* Hannah got out of the car and walked into the building without looking back. She was still angry that he'd grounded her last week.

Ben pushed the button to roll down the windows. "I love you, sweetheart," he yelled after her. The day was turning into pure shit. He made an illegal U-turn and headed towards home. Damn Maddy and her early morning meeting. She was drinking coffee somewhere in Dorchester, while he ran the kids all over town.

Holding the *Boston Globe* over his head, Ben ran into the house and up the stairs, rain and sweat slicked on his face. The hot, stuffy bedroom stifled him.

Stacks of papers and folders were scattered over, under, and next to the bed. He spread the piles over the wrinkled bed covers, throwing files one on top of another until he found what he needed. He opened the yellow folder and flipped through the pages. Yellow for administration, red for active cases, blue for fiscal, green for research, purple for political stuff and brown for general crap that didn't go anywhere else. Maybe he'd tell his secretary to start a new category: black for who gives a shit.

There. He'd found it. Finally, one small victory. Highlighter marked what he needed.

Three minutes later Ben barely looked in his rearview mirror as he slammed out of the driveway. He turned on the radio as he pulled onto the Jamaicaway, punching buttons until he hit Anthrax. Pounding music calmed him, something Maddy never understood. It knocked out the crap he dealt with all day.

He pulled ahead of the tired Plymouth in front of him. The traffic made him want to blow his brains out. Half-winding back road, half-speedway; no one knew how to drive the Jamaicaway. Ben wove in and out of traffic, another thing that made Maddy crazy.

There was just too much about Ben, Maddy didn't like.

The road became bumper to bumper. Ben crawled fifteen minutes to go half a mile and no way out, another reason for hating the piece of shit road. Ben punched stations, hitting a commercial on BCN for Saturn, piece of shit cars they were. BBC time on NPR. Pompous Brits—he hated their pretentious voices. He hit the CD button and pumped up the volume.

Ben cranked up the volume. A Buick Regal blocking his view seemed unaware he wasn't in a parking lot. Ben honked the horn a few more times. Regal crawled toward the rotary's mouth, Ben on his tail.

Cars spilled into the four-way from every direction. Regal got in first position and stopped. *There's your opening, idiot. GO.*

Ben blasted the horn this time, joined by the growing line behind him. He squeezed to the right, cutting off a car from behind. Cars streamed around the circle. Ben forced his way in, watching the Regal in the rearview, still stuck there, the wallflower of cars.

A Ford Expedition barreled down his right side. Pressing his foot down hard, Ben accelerated, but so did the Expedition. Humongous piece of crap. Ben sped up, but just as he was clear to pass, the Expedition cut him off. Metal scraped metal as Ben's left fender hit the bastard's right rear. Ben tried to straighten out, hit a slick spot, and spun out of control.

Cars heading into the rotary squealed, maneuvering away, as he crashed into the unlucky car in his path.

He hit it hard, bounced, and finally, came to a stop.

Sweat poured from him as he coughed. His rapid shallow breaths jabbed his left side as he tried to open the jammed door. The sharp smell coming from the deflated airbag burned his eyes and throat. Someone knocked on the window. The man peering through the glass looked about seventy, his short-sleeved white shirt spotted with rain. Ben nodded, letting the guy know he was alive.

Salty blood trickled from where he'd bitten his lower lip. His chest was sore where he'd snapped against the seatbelt. He lowered the jammed window as far as he could, holding his breath against the pain each time he pressed the button.

"Can you help me out?" Ben asked.

The man shook his head. "Sorry, son. Best to stay put and wait for the medics."

"Just reach in and unlock the door, okay?"

"I don't know." The man slowly stood from his crouch. A woman standing behind the old guy leaned in.

"You shouldn't move. You might have internal injuries." She pushed back the wet hair on her forehead. As though offering a condolence prize, she held up a phone. "Do you want me to call someone for you? Do you want to make a call?"

He studied the phone and the chubby wet woman. "Could you call my wife? Don't scare her. If she doesn't answer, say it's a very small accident and I'll call her as soon as I know what's up. If she answers, I'll try to talk to her."

Remembering Maddy's cell number was a good sign, he thought. Nauseous and dizzy, he hung his pounding head down as far as possible, morning coffee pressing on his bladder. He closed his eyes, and then when the spinning started, opened them. Sirens sounded closer and closer.

"She didn't answer. Anyone else you'd like me to call?" The woman looked so earnest. He could see her telling the story to her family at dinner as she served the salad: *And then I called his family for him.*

Ben rattled off his office number, feeling sticking pains as he spoke.

He'd just tried closing his eyes again when a husky young voice urged him to open them. A smoker's voice. Was it fashionable for young women to smoke now? He'd better keep an eye on Hannah.

"Sir. My name is Evanne. I'm an emergency medical worker.

Can you hear me?" The woman was light-skinned, her beaded braids pulled back into a thick yellow elastic band.

Ben opened his eyes. "I need to get out of here."

"Just a few moments, I promise. Are you allergic to latex?" When he shook his head no, she reached in and took his wrist with rubber-gloved fingers. "Can you feel that?"

He nodded. A fireman wedged a bar into the door and popped it open. By the time she'd asked what Ben weighed and what day it was, he felt as though he might faint. His hands shook as he tried to climb out of the seat, legs trembling so hard he worried they'd fold under him.

"Don't worry," Evanne said. "It's shock. Normal after a trauma. Just sit, I'll get someone to help."

Staying in the car seemed fine. Or he could just lie down in the road. Evanne and a police officer guided him a few steps toward a portable cot where he sat, hands spread on either side of the narrow slab of foam, barely managing to stay upright, his exhaustion suddenly profound.

"Why don't you lie down, sir," Evanne suggested, her throaty voice soothing.

"No. No. I'm all right."

"Really, it would be better to just lie back for now."

He was afraid to let go. Already it seemed as though fate had simply picked him up and thrown him on the ground.

"I'm master of my fate."

"What?" Evanne took his wrist in her hand.

Had he spoken aloud? The paramedic looked concerned. He supposed he'd frightened her. When she took his chin in her hands and looked into his eyes, her breath was mild peppermint, her hands lemons scented. Maybe she wasn't a smoker. Ben pictured her life, showering with yellow soap, buying Lifesavers, not knowing what each day would bring. Broken bodies. Guns. Him.

"Sorry. Guess I'm a little shook," he said.

"It's fine." She kept a comforting or controlling hand on his arm. Either way it felt good.

Bright orange cones held cars back. A barely moving line of traffic crept around the accident scene. He turned his head to the left, pain shooting through his upper back. The Expedition was ahead about fifteen yards. Even seated the young man in the front seat seemed tall. He sat sideways, legs hanging out, one big hand cradling a phone, the other covering his free ear to block out sound. Dark black shades, despite the rain, covered his eyes. He looked okay, but his back fender was smashed in pretty good. Shards from the backlights were scattered over the asphalt. Expedition had his own EMT next to him. A white guy. Older. Probably didn't smell of lemon and peppermints.

Careful, his back stiffening, something jabbing him each time he breathed, Ben turned slowly to the right, searching for the car he'd hit. Lights from three ambulances made kaleidoscopic patterns in the growing puddles.

Wet broken glass reflected in the ambulance lights. The compact car was folded as though someone had tried to smash it into too small a parking space. The driver's door was crumpled metal and a bent frame.

He reached for Evanne's hand; it seemed impossible someone had actually been in that smashed car.

A red briefcase, open, papers strewn over the road, had landed about twenty yards from the car. Ben felt light headed. He squinted through the rain. Two men laid a woman on a backboard. A red sandal dangled from her right foot, her left was bare.

Dirt streaked the woman's blood-covered blouse and blue skirt. Ben looked at the wrecked car and then turned back to see the woman again. The men wheeled her still body toward a waiting ambulance. As they positioned the stretcher to enter the ambulance, the woman's face became visible.

Jesus, Mary, and Joseph, please, no.

Under the oxygen mask was Maddy, the grey pallor of her skin visible even through the rain.

III. Hannah

Hannah waited for Caro to finish changing her clothes, anxious to get out of the dank camp locker room. She'd been on guard since seeing water rats by the nearby wharf. She acted brave when her campers were around, but alone, her stomach jumped in a regular skittish rhythm.

"I can't go with you. I'm grounded, remember?" Hannah threw her backpack over one shoulder.

"Can't you at least get ice cream?" Caro pulled a tight white tee shirt over her head, muffling her tentative voice. Her sentences always ended on a rising note—as though questioning everything.

Hannah gave a dramatic sigh. "No. My mother's picking me up, and I don't even know exactly when. I called her cell like three times, but she hasn't called back. I guess I'm supposed to wait forever, no matter what. I just exist for them, right?"

They walked down towards the beach wall. Two joggers ran by, almost knocking down a toddler holding a plastic bucket. The morning rain had been replaced by a cool dry wind. Afternoon sunlight slanted over the gritty city beach, blurring the trash and grey-black tones of the sand.

"Wait with me?" Hannah asked, as she climbed up on the wall.

"Sorry. No can do," Caro said. "Everyone's waiting. Should I tell Noah to meet you here?"

"That's just what I need, my mother driving up and finding me talking to Noah. She hasn't even met him yet."

Hannah could imagine the third degree. *Where do you live, what do your parents do, how much did you weigh when you were born?"*

"Just tell him I had to go home, okay?" Hannah waved her friend off, and then rummaged in her bag until she found a pack of almonds. Her mother threw this stuff at her, making sure she didn't starve to death. Did she think they lived in Darfur?

Hannah watched the stupid boys showing off—battling each other to be the first to knock each other off the beach wall, then looking to see if Hannah was watching. The doggy smell of the sand they'd kicked up mixed with the odor of her tee shirt. She brought her arm up to her nose and sniffed. Fried sweat.

Salty nut dust coated Hannah's mouth. She jumped down from the wall and walked to the fountain in the square. Three boys about Gracie's age took turns holding the water pressure down and spraying each other.

"Excuse me," she said.

They turned to her with a *whaddya want* look.

"Do you mind?" She gestured toward the spigot. "I think it's meant for people to get a drink."

They moved back. Slowly, but moving. She bent over the fountain, taking her time. The warm water was gross, but at least it washed the salt off her tongue.

"Hannah!" Her brother's screech filled the entire plaza.

Hannah looked up, wiping her mouth with the bottom of her tee shirt. She didn't see her mother's car.

"HANNAH!"

She blocked the sun with her hand and looked toward Caleb's voice. She heard him, but she still couldn't see her mother or the car.

"*Hannah*! Over here, darling." Grandma Anne stepped out of her blue Volvo and waved over the car roof at her.

Hannah hurried over. "What are you doing here, Grandma?"

"Mommy's hurt," Gracie whispered out the window, as though it were a secret. "But she's not going to die. Grandma said."

Hannah opened the passenger door and got into the empty seat. Her grandmother slid back behind the wheel. "What happened?"

"Put on your seat belt," her grandmother said. "Mommy was in a car accident. Daddy also."

"Daddy only had a bruised stomach." Gracie held a knuckle to her mouth, talking around it. "He's not in a room."

"She means a bruised rib. He hasn't been admitted." Her grandmother took a deep breath. "They're both going to be just fine. Just fine."

"How did it happen? Is Mom hurt bad?"

"It's all a little confusing, darling."

"But she's alright isn't she?"

"I'm sure she'll be fine," her grandmother said.

"Does she have to stay there?"

"We'll find out when we get to the hospital. I'm sure it will be okay." Grandma's voice shook. Hannah didn't know what else to ask.

Her grandmother reached into the pocket of her blue skirt and handed Hannah a pile of Wet Naps. "Wipe your face, you'll feel better. Give some to Caleb and Gracie. Everyone should cool off."

Hannah handed one to each of the kids. In unison, they opened the little foil packets wiped the alcohol-saturated squares over their faces. Her grandmother started up the car.

#

At eight, Hannah, Gracie, and Caleb were still in the main lobby, huddled in hard plastic chairs. One after another, sad-looking and sick people hunched over with pain walked through the hospital door. Some of them were too scary to even look at—the ones with bags of fluid on poles, or with swollen faces that looked about to burst. Other people carried bright gift bags, plants, and piles of magazines, their faces all pinched up.

Caleb's head lay in Hannah's lap, Gracie leaned against her other side. Her grandmother and father were somewhere conferring with the doctor about her mother. Grandma used that word— conferring. Daddy wanted them to go home with Aunt Julia, but Julia wouldn't leave the hospital. Hannah didn't want to leave. She was worried about her father too, even though when she saw him for five minutes hours ago, he said he was fine and it was nothing. He'd been walking all bent up and wrapped in bandages—so how could it be nothing.

"Is Mommy going to die?" Caleb's voice was muffled by his thumb.

"No, of course not. Don't be a jerk." Hannah smoothed down his hair.

"But she could, right?" he insisted. "It's possible."

Gracie sat up. Marks from Hannah's shirt seams lined her face. "Is it?" she asked. "Could Mommy die, Hannah?"

Gracie's face contorted with the effort to keep from crying. Her eyes were already swollen from hours of tears; Hannah had finally told her they'd be sent home if she didn't stop.

"She's not going to die," she had said. "We just have to be good. And pray." Hannah didn't know why she said that, but she didn't know what else to offer them. She had laced her fingers and pressed her palms together.

Gracie's mouth moved silently again, her hands clasped too. Caleb picked at his bandages. None of them had received anything resembling religious training, unless you counted having Passover at one set of grandparents and Easter at the other's.

Should she pray to the Easter Bunny? Hannah found herself making secret little crosses on her chest, just like Gracie, trying to make deals with God. Hannah would never disobey her parents, ever, if He just kept her mother alive. She'd take care of everyone and never be mean. *Baruch ata Adonoi Eloheinu,* she chanted in her head. Hannah didn't know what the words meant, but her mother repeated them each year as she lit the Chanukah candles. *Baruch ata Adonoi Eloheinu, please keep my mother alive.*

"But she could," Caleb repeated. "Mommy could die."

"Don't you dare say that, or I'll send you to Aunt Julia's house."

"You can't do that. Aunt Julia's here."

"Uncle Sean is there. I'll put you in a cab and send you over right now."

"You're not the boss."

"Yes I am," Hannah said. "I'm the boss until Daddy or Grandma comes back. And imagine what Daddy will do if I tell him you're saying scary things about Mommy."

Caleb got up and went to a muddy brown bench away from Hannah and Gracie. He crossed his arms and started kicking the wooden slats with his heels.

"Caleb, stop or they'll throw us out of here." Her brother looked up; his dark brown eyes reminded Hannah of war-orphans in *Newsweek.* "Come back here."

He shook his head, not looking at her, using his blue camp tee shirt to wipe underneath his eyes.

"Come back." Hannah patted the seat next to her. "I'll get you a candy bar."

Caleb shuffled back, climbed up on the couch, and put his head back on Hannah's lap. "Reese's Pieces?" He snuck his right thumb near his mouth and rubbed it against his lower lip.

"Sure. Reese's Piece's."

Fifteen minutes later, when her father came again, it seemed like they'd been waiting for fifteen hours.

"I can't stay long," he said as he sat next to Gracie. "I need to get back upstairs." He handed a twenty-dollar bill to Hannah. "Do you know where the cafeteria is?"

"Can we see Mommy?" Gracie asked.

"She's in surgery. Then she'll be in intensive care."

"Why is she being operated on?" Hannah asked.

"She has some head injuries. It's complicated, honey. We'll talk later. Mommy will be fine," he repeated.

"How do they operate on her head?" Caleb asked when their father left.

Hannah reached over and pulled Caleb on her lap, pressing her cheek to his thin back. "Mommy will be fine. Like Daddy said."

Baruch ata Adonoi Eloheinu, please keep my mother alive.

- The End -

POETRY

Art

~

Ysabel de la Rosa

You Prune the Bonsai
in the extra room, and no
one knows, save the tree

You release the shears
to float to floor and then see
trunk and branches bow

No one else knows, no
one else watches or believes,
just you and the tree

Just you and the tree
practicing eternity
in the extra room

One More Day

J.D. Blair

Give me just one more day near the honeysuckle on the James River in August, for sex before breakfast and the bouquet of early morning love and a day watching Pacific sunsets stratify as they melt through the atmosphere along the Big Sur and the feel of sea salt skin on the beach or one day on old embarcadero in Morro Bay embracing the beach house warmth and another fishing the Merced in Tuolumne Meadows and angling high lakes for trout starving for any fly and another day in the fog of Golden Gate Park with eucalyptus dripping, and a day biking the foothills of the Pyrenees and another sharing with "Lefty" the three legged squirrel and "Lock Jaw" the aging blue jay, just one more day.

Ginna in the Silence

Ginna Wilkerson

Whispers from the trees speak welcome silence
Woody, soft-flesh souls grow in the silence.

Solid earth can feel like wavering space
The trick is stepping safe in careful silence.

Chattering raindrops fall on sizzling pavement
The end of endless rain is grateful silence.

Secrets blowing in the wind relieve my pain
Nobody knows how much I love the silence.

My ears are often closed to shameless truth
Shame can rest in peace within the silence.

I long to know the subtleties of trees
Catch words adrift on accidental silence.

"Ginna" sounds so green and growing – peaceful
Speak my name, but don't disturb the silence.

La Specola

Stephanie A. Amsel

She became a spectacle
people tittered and pointed
as she dragged around
her bag of flies

Large iridescent horseflies
fresh from dung heaps

African tsetse flies
ready to gorge
on a camel
or a woman
squatting in the sand

Small house flies
abdomens sweet and full
of pomegranates and figs

She selected her prey
one by one
carefully
picked her enemies
to receive the bites
the poison of
her calculated strikes

But there was a hole
in the bag and all
the flies were set free
many eyes opened wide

The victims walked along
Intact and unaware

Elegy of the Witness - The Same River Twice

Piero Scaruffi

The shining spires of Istanbul
disappear under the lunar pollen
that the dervishes evoked
with their feverish dances.
The day is dismantled
only to be reassembled
less different tomorrow.
Bats dye jagged orbits
into the mesh of a bleeding
sky, like kites torn apart
by wicked whirlwinds.
I waded through the stillness
past a concert of flickering candles
lulling the thin layer of shadows
at the edge of the bridge, and faded
into the cold wind of the strait
where the lights morphed into the city,
one man waltzing with his ghost
the dance they never danced back home.

Do these stars return nightly
to show us something
that we've always failed to see?
Are these stars the same
reflections that twinkled
in your eyes at the beach?

Is this world the same creature
that looked so small next to you?
Night turns the heart into a stage
where our drama can be reenacted

without fear of reciting the lines
that we spent a lifetime rehearsing.

Why am i here tonight
if not to feel the distance
and long for what i left behind?

Let Your Soul Rise

~

J. George Hume

They say that your mother was Communist, and you often spoke of singing your own national anthem in dimmed rooms praising the Russian flag, while burning the stars and stripes. They say you once told a woman, after she made pass after pass, you would meet the next night at some hotel bar in the Village. You never showed.

Yet your soul continued to fly, even after the police came, taking you away into the night after you swore that it was okay to hide millions of stolen goods in your apartment and that you were insane, sending you to Rockland, your world upside down, wishing, dreaming, that Neal would come magically in a car and drive away with you into the setting Pacific sun.

And you continued to sing the songs of confusion and above poet angst. Even against the pounding fists on your door from a distant but related Uncle Sam, who wanted you to enlist, who wanted you to speak of the underworld that you belonged to, that wanted you to watch Walter Cronkite and the Brady Bunch over cookies and milk. You knew though, you knew, you had something they could never touch or take, and you wrote clearly, "All my poems are published in Heaven".

And your soul continued to rise, and you met God, and asked Him why your mother was treated the way she was. Why they buried her wrongly, and shamed her name and you made peace with Him, over a donut, two pitchers of lysergic acid and a Kaddish.

And your soul never came down, even after fellow Beatniks, Tim Leary, even Carl Solomon, closed their eyes and stopped muttering passages of Whitman. How I, after reading Howl and America, wished to see you appear on top of the Broadway hill in North Beach, sipping tea and asking if I knew where Lawrence was. I would've hugged you, recited the end of Sun Flower Sutra, and asked if you take me with you anywhere, including the sky. but your soul was still flying. Flying, even after your name stopped making the Times, even after you stopped walking around City Lights, even after you died Allen, even after you died, your radiating sea beam myopia mantra golden sun shining ripened free of chains permanently newly born victorious supernova carrying soaring soul is still dancing.

Maudie and Claude

~

Floyd E. Batchelder

Oh, Gloria, damn, would that you had been along!
Well, no, it had to be only Claude and me
and like no other Thames can ever be,
except I'd done a better sonnet, all rhymey,
as Edmund Spens' "Spring Come, Winter Gone"
if a gin I'd had instead my Irish tea.

'Twas brillig, you know, a real bravo,
with a one and a two of Heineken's brew,
trees blossoming, flowers abloom,
breezy, a taddish cold, April in our eyes,
great bottles of green jolly and Queen's fun.

Claude? I'd known him as a lad--
hadn't seen him in 40 years!
then bumped him a week Friday in a dart game;
and now, a dream week past, we're on the Thames,
water all pollen fuzzy and cozy green.
"Spring turns the algae over," says Claude,
high on the pole at his end o' the punt--
the grand guy, dressed punk larky, a laughing joke,
striped shirt, green galluses, pancake hat.
Me at full punt at my end, silky blue,
twirling a yellow parasol that came with the punt,
dodging it up and down, peekabooing around.

He had given me--beyond the asking and the taking out--
a heart-stopping basket of flowers,
not part of the punt, but for me, for me alone!
Five pounds he had handed the man,
above the buying of the Heinekens.

The basket in my lap, I'm tossing flowers,
poet-queen o' the Thames, smiling at Claude,
telling him with eyes and bobbing buds
that I'm blooming happy.

The punt ashore and fixed to a tree,
we stopped at noon at Farthinton's
for lunch and highest tea,
walking, your Lord and Ladylike, across the mall;
Claude, holding me delicately the parasol:

A finnan haddie we had, my Claude and me,
Done exquisite fine in orange and tarty lime;
We dined, as Edmund 'ave said, "no thought o' time,"
'Til the waiter plattered us the check at three--
Leaving our toasty glasses ruddy empty.
The waiter, at sideboards pulling faces,
Was counting spoons as Claude moved round my side--
Arm 'bout me--when out of silver chalices,
Out of the chandelier and empty glasses,
Claude bold did ask me marry him--he did! he did!
Yes! I said--heart jump-ahump--no haws, no hems;
Yes! I said next breath, so wondrous our Thames,
So much more marvelous than Edmund Spens'
Antique line and perfect rhyme, my Claude, my Thames.

Three Poems

~

Valerie Stokes

~

November

Gone
the stark white
reality
of wild roses
under moonlight
sprigs of pine
raspberries
piled high
topped
with fresh
whipped cream
in Dresden
on sun-stained lace
and the pale blue
china cups
bearing perfect
brews of coffee
are now
the ghostly grays
of autumn

Rarely a morning
still exists
when things
seem new
In quiet protest

I conjure places
of wonder
where you are
dancing me down
sidewalks
of first hellos
whirling me dizzy
into the night

I lift my cup
my darling
and drink you
renewing
all yesterdays
tomorrows
days between
each season
every poem
written
in some
street corner
cafe
and should
November
come again
I shall
wish for you

Writer's Block

The air
is fresh brewed
Earl Grey
and flaming steaks
topped with eggs
to order
served with
nine-year cheddar
and well-stocked
breadbaskets

I want
the window seat
near the far edge
of the room
where the sun
slashes
at the long shadows
of everything
it touches
scattering patterns
of early
morning light
from ceiling to floor
into showers
of crimson bloom

But today
the server
all nose rings
and baubles
intent on spooning
indifference
and saccharine
into my tea
hovers

like a dragonfly
demanding attention
with mantras
and even the cocky
and serious masses
drown out
the clattering
of silver
against porcelain

With all
the excitement
and eagerness
of writing gone awry
I sit a voyeur
sipping my tea
embraced within
the confines
of rumpled collars
cornrows and cowlicks
bouffant and French nails
buried deep
in the eclectic whir
of laughter
old spice
and stale smoke
drifting to where
one sweet music
might have been

My River and Forest

For Heather

I still remember
Summer afternoons
And those funny faces -
Friends
Running wild
Shoeless
In their games
I hear
Glissandos of laughter
Smell the innocence
Of lilacs leafing
And swallowtails looping
Like brilliant blue
Pansies afloat
In the slightest
Puff of air

Frog ponds
Cottonwoods
Fiddlehead ferns
Spreading luxuriantly
In pilloried
Drifts of light
Milkweed
Spidery with webs
The mournful aria
Of the screech owl
Its soft-gray tufts
Anchored
In morning mist
The swirling waters
Deliciously cool
At my feet

It was my wilderness

Where I went to dream
At the water's edge
My Monet
Warm lullaby
Lush new Eden
Where locusts
Wandered aimless
And I was hopelessly lost
In fresh air
And sun-ripened
Reverie

There were fox trails
Dusty paths
To the graveyard
Of a old cabin
Abandoned
Broken
One wall missing
And if I was lucky
I would peek inside
At the elusiveness
Of dark-eyed hares
Belching clover
And ring-tailed
Raccoons hidden away
Somewhere
Within a virtual
Bag of tricks

And oh
How the maples and aspens
Played the clown
Daring to dream
Carnivals of coppery
Reds and ochre
And plucked apples
Tasted sweeter
Than any
I had ever known

Now a brief music

Except for the rustlings
Of finger leaves
In another time

February Morning, Vashon Island

Anthony Russell White

Fluttery gray shapes fly low
over flat Puget Sound.

A drop of rain trying to get home.

Offshore a pod of orcas feeds
on migrating Chinook salmon.

In my dream you came naked
bearing gifts, hand-made letters
from every cousin, offering a
special favor or task—whatever
they knew or did best. Your
breasts shown with the dawn
light, and your smile was the
smile of contentment.

Deep in the mud the razor clams
siphon food from the tidal surge.

A fisherman, alone in his boat with the light.

What if everything you ever dreamed of
waited in a hidden room just beyond this wall?

About The Authors

Beverly Akerman has had stories published recently in *Red Wheelbarrow, The Nashwaak Review* and *Rio Grande Review*, and will soon appear in *Descant*. She lives in Montreal with her husband and 3 children. After two decades in molecular genetics research, she has just quit her day job.

Stephanie Amsel is a doctoral student at The University of Texas at San Antonio, studying creative writing and Italian and English medieval literature. She also teaches fourth grade at a public elementary school in San Antonio. Stephanie writes fiction and poetry. Her poetry has been published in *Sagebrush Review*.

Angela Kriger Blackwood graduated from Louisiana State University with a degree in English Literature and commissioned in the US Air Force in 2004. She is currently working on a novel, as well as co-editing and contributing to a collection of memoirs from women serving in the military. She now resides in Fife, Washington with her husband and two dogs.

J.D. Blair writes short fiction, poetry and essays. His story "The Downer" will appear in *Orchid* where it won their short, short fiction competition. His short story "Charlotta's Wake" appeared in a recent issue of *Homestead Review*. He lives in Walnut Creek, California with his wife Floy, two cats and a dove.

Ysabel de la Rosa has appeared in various publications including: *Calyx, Nimrod, Oregon East, Fishquake, The Amherst Review* and *Connecticut Review*. Her poem *Inside the Circle* was a finalist for the 2006 Pablo Neruda Poetry Award.

Gilda Haber is a native of London. She has about 35 publications ranging from scholarly to racy. Her story *Tea with the Editor* is a chapter from her manuscript *Cockney Girl,* as yet unpublished in toto. Gilda teaches sociology, writing and literature at Montgomery College. She resides in Maryland.

J. George Hume has competed in poetry slams in Boston, reading the Beats in the upstairs floor of City Lights, or reciting at Sweeties. He continued the pursuit of his passion through his studies at Trinity College in Connecticut, and currently through writing and reading his works live in venues around San Francisco. Currently, George is the Associate Alliance Manager for Latin America and the Caribbean at salesforce.com. George divides his time between his home in San Francisco and the home of his extended family in Sanitago, Chile.

Ruth Lilian has had her work published in *Literal Latte, New Press* and *Writer's Digest,* where she won their International Short Story Competition. She is the author of a One-Act play and was a finalist for the *Heekin Foundation* fellowships program; *James Jones Fellowship*; *Southern Anthology*, and the *Southern Priz.e.* She lives in New Jersey.

Randy Susan Meyers has taught at Boston's Grub Street Writers' Center, where she is an active member. Her published work includes the co-authored nonfiction book *Couples with Children*, which was excerpted in *Self Magazine, New Parent's Advisor,* and *Expecting Magazine.* Her short story, *Mixed Prayers*, links excerpts from her newly finished novel.

Sharon Mortz is originally from upstate New York and turned to writing in 2001 when her daughter died. She has been published in various magazines including *FATE.* Sharon currently resides in San Francisco.

Michael John Paul Pope just completed his debut novel, *Bed of God.* His second novel, *Ghost Walking* is well under way. Michael lives in New Jersey with his wife and two children.

Lynn Veach Sadler has published widely in academics and creative writing. Editor, poet, fiction/creative nonfiction writer, and playwright, she has a full-length poetry collection forthcoming from RockWay Press. One story appears in Del Sol's *Best of 2004 Butler Prize Anthology*; another won the 2006 Abroad Writers Contest/Fellowship (France). *Not Your Average Poet* (on Robert Frost) was a *Pinter Review* Prize for Drama Silver Medalist in 2005.

Jackie Shannon-Hollis lives in Portland, Oregon and has completed a collection of short stories and begun work on a novel. Her work has appeared in *MARY, Rosebud, The South Dakota Review, The Oregon Literary Review, Fiction Attic, flashquake,* and *Inkwell.*

Valerie Stokes has returned to writing over the last two years. She shares her life with those who share her passion for words. In times of doubt, Valerie finds inspiration from family and friends. Always, she'll write about people she knows, and those great writers she's never met that are the keepers of stars.

Donna Trump attended Northwestern University in Illinois where she received undergraduate degrees in Biology and Physical Therapy. After a brief career as a physical therapist, a longer stint as an over-involved mother, she took her first creative writing class at The Loft Literary Center in Minneapolis. She was selected as one of four emerging fiction writers to participate in The Loft's 2007-2008 Mentor Series.

Anthony Russell White serves on the permanent staff of the Nine Gates Mystery School. A poetic high point for him was a visit to the tomb of Jelaluddin Rumi at Konya, Turkey in 1994; he is still awed by Rumi's poetry. William Stafford has been another major influence. White admires the way his quiet, plain language still manages to go quite deep in a few lines.

Ginna Wilkerson is a doctoral student in literature at the University of South Florida in Tampa. She has had poems featured online by *Poetry Soup* and *Cedar Hill Press* and published in an anthology by *Inkpot Press.* Her poem *Ceremony* will appear in the fall 2007 edition of *Gertrude.*